Elite • 73

OSPREY
PUBLISHING

D1283594

American Civil War Commanders (1)

Union Leaders in the East

Philip Katcher • Illustrated by Richard Hook

Series editor Martin Windrow

First published in Great Britain in 2002 by Osprey Publishing,
Elms Court, Chapel Way, Botley, Oxford OX2 9LP, United Kingdom.
Email: **info@ospreypublishing.com**

ISBN 1 84176 320 9
Editor: Martin Windrow
Design: Alan Hamp
Index by Alan Thatcher
Originated by Grasmere Digital Imaging, Leeds, UK
Printed in China through World Print Ltd.

02 03 04 05 06   10 9 8 7 6 5 4 3 2 1

FOR A CATALOGUE OF ALL BOOKS PUBLISHED BY
OSPREY MILITARY AND AVIATION PLEASE CONTACT:
The Marketing Manager, Osprey Direct UK
PO Box 140, Wellingborough, Northants
NN8 4ZA, United Kingdom
Email: **info@ospreydirect.co.uk**

The Marketing Manager, Osprey Direct USA
c/o Motorbooks International, PO Box 1
Osceola, WI 54020-0001, USA
Email: **info@ospreydirectusa.com**

www.ospreypublishing.com

Author's Note

For reasons of space it seems appropriate to divide the commanders
to be covered in this and a forthcoming second volume between the
"Eastern" and "Western" theaters of war, according to their first,
most imporant or best-known operations. Inevitably, given the
movement of some generals between the theaters, this has worked
more neatly in some cases than in others, whose placing in one or
other title has necessarily been somewhat arbitrary. Readers should
regard the two books together as a single reference source.

Acknowledgments

All monochrome illustrations in this book are from the collection of
Military Images magazine.

Artist's Note

Readers may care to note that the original paintings from which the
colour plates in this book were prepared are available for private
sale. All reproduction copyright whatsoever is retained by the
Publishers. All enquiries should be addressed to:

Scorpio Gallery, PO Box 475, Hailsham, E.Sussex BN27 2SL

The Publishers regret that they can enter into no correspondence
upon this matter.

OPPOSITE **The brash, self-confident Joseph Hooker, seen
here while still a brigadier-general, would be appointed to
command the Army of the Potomac in December 1862. He
lost his nerve, and the battle, at Chancellorsville the
following May. Sent West, he regained his reputation with
the public but not with his fellow generals, who never
trusted him – he had a reputation for insincerity and
back-biting behind his affable manner.**
    **The mid-19th-century photographic process points up the
contrast of the dark blue velvet collar and cuffs against the
cloth of his coat; he wears a crimson line officer's sash.
Note the hilt of the staff officer's sword, with a general
officer's gold cord knot.**

AMERICAN CIVIL WAR COMMANDERS (1) UNION LEADERS IN THE EAST

INTRODUCTION

THE ORGANIZATION OF THE United States Army in 1861 was based on the needs of a nation basically at peace, with no borders to guard against an aggressive enemy, and a traditional national distrust of large standing armies. The army had no units larger than a regiment, and even these regiments rarely came together as a single force, being largely dispersed among many separate and often remote forts in company strength. As a result the army felt no need for any rank higher than a major-general, while brigadier-generals would command brigades assembled on an as-needed basis. The senior general, who had been Winfield Scott for as long as most Americans could remember, was designated the Major-General Commanding the Army, but he was the only man ever to hold this particular rank.

Generals usually came from the ranks of the graduates of the US Military Academy at West Point, New York (Winfield Scott, who had been appointed directly before the War of 1812, was an exception). At West Point they received instruction enabling them to obtain a degree in engineering – a skill needed in a fast-growing country – along with basic military training in the various arms. However, after graduation from the Academy there was no system of continuing advanced schooling for the individuals who would eventually rise to become general officers.

At the same time, each state had its own militia, headed by a major-general appointed by the state governor, with brigadier-generals appointed to command largely "paper" brigades. In some cases these men had military experience, but they were just as apt to be purely political appointees.

When the Civil War broke out in 1861 it was obvious that the tiny pre-war regular army could not sustain the Union's war effort alone, especially given the fact that about one-third of that army's 1,100-odd officers chose to serve the Confederacy. New brigadier- and major-generals would be needed to command the large brigades and divisions that would be formed. These men, however, would receive only temporary rank as "generals of volunteers" rather than regular army rank. In many cases regular officers serving at much lower grades offered their services to their state governors and, because of the need for men with any degree of real military experience, were directly appointed generals of volunteers. Other generals of volunteers were appointed from state militias, often because they had been important in the minority political party and the administration felt it was important to show bipartisan support for the war.

3

The army in the field grew so large that as early as 1862 corps were formed by assembling divisions. These corps were commanded by major-generals, there being no higher rank authorized. Indeed, major-generals also commanded the field armies, and the "general-in-chief" was a major-general until Ulysses S.Grant received an appointment as lieutenant-general, a rank re-created by Congress which had last been given to George Washington.

The performance of these generals varied tremendously. A few proved to be outstanding. Some were so abysmal that they were forced out of the service early on; while others did so well that they were offered regular army commissions (often at considerably lower ranks than those they had held during the war) at the end of hostilities. Between these two extremes we find the mass of men who proved themselves more or less competent at the head of brigades, divisions, and corps. Some who acquitted themselves well at the lower levels of command were over-promoted and seem to have been overwhelmed by their increased responsibilities. Both those who rose to the challenge well, and those who were defeated by it, included pre-war professional officers and political appointees alike.

One quality which most shared – a quality whose absence was quickly noticed, and was not tolerated, by their contemporaries – was physical courage. On the battlefields of the 1860s general officers were expected routinely to expose themselves to the dangers faced by their men, and many paid with their lives and limbs. (Of the 28 generals whose careers are described in this book, ten were wounded in action at least once and three were killed.)

George McClellan (the short figure sixth from left – he was only about 5ft.4ins. tall) meets President Abraham Lincoln after the bloody battle of Antietam in September 1862. The figure central between McClellan and Lincoln is Fitz John Porter; George A.Custer, then a subaltern on McClellan's staff, stands far right next to the tent flap, wearing a tall-crowned slouch hat.

Sherman on staffs

Each general was allowed a staff to help him exercise command. One of the Union's leading generals, William T. Sherman, wrote about staffs after the war, based on his experience:

"I don't believe in a chief of staff at all, and any general commanding an army, corps, or division, that has a staff-officer who professes to know more than his chief, is to be pitied. Every regiment should have a competent adjutant, quartermaster, and commissary, with two or three medical officers. Each brigade commander should have the same staff, with the addition of a couple of young aides-de-camp, habitually selected from the subalterns of the brigade, who should be good riders, and intelligent enough to give and explain the orders of their general.

"The same staff will answer for a division. The general in command of a separate army, and of a *corps d'armée*, should have the same professional assistance, with two or more good engineers, and his adjutant-general should exercise all the functions usually ascribed to a chief of staff, viz., he should possess the ability to comprehend the scope of operations, and to make verbally and in writing all the orders and details necessary to carry into effect the views of his general, as well as to keep the returns and records of events for the information of the next high authority, and for history. A bulky staff implies a division of responsibility, slowness of action, and indecision, whereas a small staff implies action and concentration of purpose. The smallness of General Grant's staff throughout the civil war forms the best model for future imitation."

BIOGRAPHIES

BARLOW, Francis Channing (1834–96)

Francis Channing Barlow (**see Plate F2**) was born in Brooklyn, New York, on 19 October 1834. His father was a minister, and he was raised in his mother's hometown of Brookline, Massachusetts. Barlow was a member of the Harvard graduating class of 1855, after which he went to New York to study law. Admitted to the bar in 1858, he was in practice there until the outbreak of the Civil War.

He joined the 12th Regiment, New York State Militia as a private in the heat of passion that followed the Confederate attack on Fort Sumter. The next evening, 20 April 1861, he married Arabella Griffith at St Paul's Chapel. He joined out of love of his country, and after the war he would write: "No one rejoices more than myself in the overcoming of a rebellion the design of which was to destroy this Government for the purpose of maintaining the monstrous institution of slavery."

Barlow would not remain a private for long. Within two weeks of enlisting he had been commissioned a first lieutenant in the regiment's engineer company. He was mustered out at the end of the regiment's term of three months' service; and was then appointed lieutenant-colonel of the 61st New York Infantry. One of his soldiers later wrote that Barlow "was not at first sight an impressive looking officer. He was of medium height, of slight build, with a pallid countenance, and a weakish drawling voice. In his movements there was an appearance of loose jointedness and an absence of prim stiffness."

Rapidly promoted to colonel, he led the 61st throughout the Peninsula campaign. In battle there he proved his personal heroism, and demanded the same from his soldiers. In the Seven Days' fighting (25 June–1 July 1862), at the head of his regiment as it moved up to the line, he came across several unarmed, skulking Federal soldiers. "I spoke to several and asked them why they did not go on. They said they had lost their guns," he wrote. "I pointed them out to my men as examples of what a coward is." He praised the conduct of his own men once they got into action, saying that "The greater part of the men stood firm and erect during the firing, and only stooped or went down when ordered to do so… ."

At Antietam (17 September 1862) he was severely wounded but, two days later, his service was recognised by appointment as a brigadier-general of volunteers. He was given command of a brigade in XI Corps which, at Chancellorsville

Engraved portrait of Francis Barlow from the 9 July 1864 issue of *Harper's Weekly*. He wears a somewhat oversized custom-made fatigue blouse or "sack coat", with the single star of a brigadier-general on the front of his forage cap. According to to the paper, "Throughout the [1864] campaign Barlow is conspicious among the noble band of united heroes, officers and men, in the very active front of the battle." Badly wounded at both Antietam and Gettysburg, this pale, slightly built 30-year-old gained his greatest success in the capture of the "Mule Shoe" salient at Spotsylvania in May 1864.

(1–6 May 1863), was driven from the field in confusion during the flank attack made by Stonewall Jackson's corps on the Union right.

In the defense of Cemetery Ridge on the first day of Gettysburg (1 July 1863) Barlow was wounded and left for dead on the field, with his arms and legs temporarily paralyzed. Years after the war the Confederate Gen. John B.Gordon described how he ran across a wounded Union officer after the first day's fighting. "Quickly dismounting and lifting his head, I gave him water from my canteen, asking his name and the character of his wounds. He was Major General Francis C.Barlow, of New York, and of Howard's corps." In fact, however, modern scholarship has proved that Gordon was not in the same part of the field as Barlow, and this story was not based in fact.

Exchanged by the Confederates, Barlow recovered in time to participate in the 1864 campaign against Lee's Army of Northern Virginia as a divisional commander in II Corps under Winfield Scott Hancock. It was during this campaign, at Spotsylvania, that he decided his troops could overrun Confederate entrenchments by a massive attack in column, without artillery preparation or any halting to fire. In the early hours of 12 May 1864, somewhat delayed by fog, his division and that commanded by David Birney smashed through the Confederate lines at the "Mule Shoe", capturing some 3,000 prisoners including two generals, 30 colors, and 20 cannon.

After a forced absence on sick leave during the siege of Petersburg, Barlow recovered and returned to the army to be active at the battle of Sailor's Creek and in the Appomattox campaign. On 25 May 1865 he was named a major-general of volunteers in recognition of his service.

After the war Barlow went into politics, twice being elected secretary of state in New York, as well as serving as a United States marshal and the state attorney general in 1871. It was in this latter position that he began the first prosecution of the politically corrupt "Tweed Ring" in New York City. He died in New York on 11 January 1896, and was buried in Brookline, Massachusetts.

BURNSIDE, Ambrose Everett (1824–81)

Ambrose Burnside (see Plate C2) was born at Liberty, Indiana, on 23 May 1824. After finishing primary school he was apprenticed to a tailor, and later became a partner in a tailor's shop in Liberty before his father was able to secure him an appointment to the US Military Academy. He was graduated from the Academy in 1847 and appointed a brevet second lieutenant in the 2nd Artillery.

As the war in Mexico was nearly finished when he graduated, his only wartime service was in the Mexico City garrison. Thereafter he served on the southwestern frontier, being wounded slightly in a skirmish with Apaches in 1849. While in the army he invented a breech-loading carbine which used a fixed brass cartridge. He resigned his commission in 1853 and went to Bristol, Rhode Island, where he gathered investors to begin manufacturing this weapon. He was, however, unable to sell it to the army. A very sociable man, Burnside was both nominated to Congress and given a job with the Illinois Central Railroad, then being run by George B.McClellan, an old army friend. Burnside also became major-general of the Rhode Island militia.

On the outbreak of war Burnside organised the 1st Rhode Island Infantry, one of the first northern regiments to march to the relief of Washington. He was there given command of a brigade, which he commanded at First Bull Run (21 July 1861). For his service he received a commission as brigadier-general of volunteers on 6 August. Burnside was friendly with President Lincoln, and received command of the expedition sent to the North Carolina coast, where he successfully made landings and set up permanent bases. For these successes he was promoted to major-general of volunteers on 18 March 1862.

Returning to the Army of the Potomac outside Washington, Burnside was given command of IX Corps at Antietam. During the battle of 17 September 1862 he moved slowly, taking precious hours to capture a bridge across Antietam Creek, which could have been forded easily at a number of points; this delay allowed Lee to concentrate his troops to face other threats. Even so, when McClellan was relieved of command for not pursuing Lee, Lincoln appointed Burnside to command the Army of the Potomac on 7 November 1862.

The army, loyal to McClellan from top to bottom, was not happy about the change. Major-General Marsena Patrick, the army's provost marshal, wrote that after Burnside took over "He appeared well – very well, but all seemed to think there was one they liked much better… ." Patrick also observed that Burnside was "rather obtuse in his conceptions & is very forgetful."

Burnside led the Army of the Potomac directly south toward Richmond, but was halted on the Rappahannock River at Fredericksburg. Losing time while pontoon bridges were brought up and

Ambrose Burnside, a West Point graduate, invented a carbine, and had left the army to organize its manufacture in Rhode Island before the war broke out. He raised a regiment immediately, which became the 1st Rhode Island, and led it to Washington, where he was soon promoted to a brigade command. Here he wears his original regimental uniform, a dark blue overshirt with gray trousers; it is intriguing to recall that his first trade was as a tailor.

The sociable and popular Burnside, here wearing regulation uniform as a major-general, became the Army of the Potomac's third commander, but – as he freely admitted – he lacked the ability for such a post. After greatly damaging the army at Fredericksburg he was demoted to command of his old IX Corps. After the war Ulysses S.Grant wrote of him: "General Burnside was an officer who was generally liked and respected. He was not, however, fitted to command an army. No one knew this better than himself. He always admitted his blunders, and extenuated those of officers under him beyond what they were entitled to. It was hardly his fault that he was ever assigned to a separate command."

emplaced, he then ordered his army into repeated frontal charges against Confederate positions on higher ground which Lee had been able to prepare while awaiting the attack (13 December 1862). The attempt was a total and very costly failure; nevertheless, Burnside wanted to lead his own IX Corps in renewed attacks the next day, finally being talked out of it by his subordinates.

He then started to move the army west along the Rappahannock to outflank Lee; but the weather turned against him, and the Army of the Potomac became mired in the mud. Unable to move, Burnside then asked Lincoln either to relieve him or to dismiss some troublesome subordinates; and the President chose to replace him with Joseph Hooker.

Burnside received command of the Department of the Ohio in March 1863, ably defending Knoxville, Tennessee, against Confederate attack – though Patrick noted, "We may look for any disaster from Burnside. He is unfit to be in any separate command."

IX Corps was brought up to strength, and Burnside resumed command and rejoined the Army of the Potomac, although directly under command of the overall army commander, U.S. Grant, for the 1864 campaign that led to the siege of Petersburg. There he proposed a disastrous attempt on Confederate lines following a huge mine explosion ("the Crater", 30 July 1864) – a mismanaged attack which cost enormous casualties. Burnside resigned on 15 April 1865.

After the war he was elected governor of Rhode Island three times, and thereafter as one of the state's senators, in which position he was serving at his death on 13 September 1881.

BUTLER, Benjamin Franklin (1818–93)

Born in Deerfield, New Hampshire on 5 November 1818, Butler (see Plate A2) graduated from Colby College in Maine in 1838. Returning to Lowell, he was admitted to the bar in 1840 and practiced criminal law as well as entering politics. He was elected to the Massachusetts legislature in 1853 and again in 1859, serving as a representative to the Democratic Convention. He endorsed Southern rights, being a supporter of the extreme States' Rights candidate, John C.Breckinridge.

Despite this position, Butler – a brigadier-general in theMassachusetts militia before the war – led his 8th Massachusetts Regiment to Washington in 1861. There, on 16 May, he was appointed a major-general of volunteers, more to indicate proof of Democratic support for putting down the Southern "rebellion" than as a testimony to his abilities. Sent to Fortress Monroe, Butler led an expedition that was defeated at Big Bethel (10 June), the first noted Union defeat of the war.

"I regret that he has not as much capacity for handling troops judiciously in the field as he has for 'managing' his superiors and kicking out his subordinates", wrote Brig.Gen. Joseph R.Hawley, who later served under Butler. "Yet I wish that some of our accomplished soldiers had some of his peculiar traits, & his knowledge of men & things generally crowded into their somewhat narrow professional minds."

While at Monroe, Butler ruled that slaves who escaped to Union lines did not have to be returned to their owners, since their use aided the Confederates and they were thus "contraband of war". Such sinuous legal reasoning was typical of the man; one of his officers would write, "Butler is sharp, shrewd, able, without conscience or modesty – overbearing. A bad man to have against you in a criminal case." Another of his officers called him astute, quick-witted, unscrupulous, and audacious. Some of his actions at Monroe were certainly questionable. He sold trade permits to civilians who did business in his department. He received kickbacks from Northern firms that sold farm implements and other goods to Southern companies that could pay in cotton. Some of this cotton may have been shipped north in army transports, loaded by army troops and stevedores.

In August 1861 Butler was sent with a force to take Hatteras Inlet, which he did successfully. In May 1862 he commanded the troops that took over New Orleans after the US Navy forced its surrender. There he ruled that women who

Benjamin Butler had been involved in the Massachusetts militia before the war, but his main interests lay in politics. It was his considerable Democrat powerbase in New England which brought him appointment as a major-general, but he proved a poor commander. It was only after the 1864 presidential election, however, when the Republicans were safely in office and the Confederacy appeared doomed, that the government felt safe in dismissing him. Note the oakleaf embroidery on his collar, a personal affectation.

BELOW This engraving from a photograph shows Butler wearing another heavily embroidered uniform, recalling that worn by Winfield Scott. Always a political animal, and widely suspected of corruption, Butler made friends with the press correspondents accompanying the army, being especially helpful to those who gave him favorable coverage. However, a positive consequence of his self-seeking character was that he also made sure that his soldiers were on his side by expediting mail to and from the front, as well as aiding the US Sanitary Commission and US Christian Commission in their work for the troops – his commands were noted for having among the best, most forward hospital facilities.

insulted Union officers were to be treated as women of the night plying their trade. The South was deeply insulted by this order, and actually placed a price on Butler's head. There, too, he gained the nickname of "Spoons Butler", it being said that he stole silver spoons, as well as other personal property, for his own benefit. Such allegations were not proved, but he was relieved of command there in December 1862.

In 1864 Butler was named commander of a new Army of the James, made up of several corps drawn from the deep South. This was intended to land at Bermuda Hundred and take Richmond from the south. In fact Confederate forces managed to entrench in his front, and those works, coupled with his indecision, halted his force as if he had been corked in a bottle. He then led a force against Fort Fisher, the last fort in the Confederacy to defend an Atlantic Coast port; this attempt failed after his plan to explode a ship full of powder did not level the fort as expected. He was recalled to New York in November 1864, and in January 1865 he was forced to resign his commission.

After Butler was gone the army appointed a commission to look into charges of corruption against him. The report they produced indicated that Butler was indeed involved in such activities, but nothing happened as a result.

Changing his affiliation to Republican, Butler was elected to Congress between 1866 and 1875 and again in 1878 (this time as a "Greenbacker"), and was elected governor in 1882. He was the Greenbacker presidential candidate in 1884, and died in Washington, DC on 11 January 1893.

CHAMBERLAIN, Joshua Lawrence (1828–1919)

Born in Brewer, Maine, on 8 September 1828, Chamberlain (see Plate H3) was educated at a military academy at Ellsworth, then graduated from Bowdoin College in 1852; finally he graduated from the Bangor Theological Seminary in 1855. He was then named a professor at Bowdoin, the post that he held when the Civil War began.

Commissioned lieutenant-colonel of the 20th Maine in August 1862, he subsequently became the unit's colonel. Given his military academy and teaching experience, he seems to have been well regarded in the regiment. Major Holman Melcher wrote home on 27 June 1863 that "Our beloved Col. Chamberlain is not able to command us owing to sickness, but he is on the recovery and we all hail the day he is able to resume his command of the regiment."

Joshua Chamberlain saw active service from Antietam to Appomattox; but it was 2 July 1863, the second day of Gettysburg, that brought him his most famous moment. Vincent's brigade was hurried to hold a position at the far left of the Union line, and the 20th Maine was posted on the extreme left of the brigade – and thus of the whole Union army – with orders to hold the commanding height of Little Round Top. Law's Alabama brigade moved against them, and Chamberlain's men held off assault after assault. Finally, with the regiment's ammunition exhausted, Chamberlain called for a bayonet assault, leading it down the hill in person against the weary Confederates (who, in fact, were preparing to retire as the 20th's charge hit them). For this action, after the war, Chamberlain was awarded the Medal of Honor. Chamberlain described his defense of Little Round Top in a letter to Maine's governor on 21 July 1863:

"We were assigned to the *extreme left* of our line of battle, where the fiercest assault was made. A whole Rebel Brigade was opposed to this Regiment, charging on us with desperate fury, in column of Regiments, so that we had to contend with a front of *fresh troops* after each struggle. After two hours fighting on the defensive, our loss had been so great, & the remaining men were so much exhausted, having fired all our 'sixty-rounds' & all the cartridges we could gather from the scattered boxes of the fallen around us, friend & foe, I saw no way left but to take the *offensive* & accordingly we charged on the enemy – trying 'cold steel' on them. The result was we drove them entirely out of the field, killing one hundred & fifty of them & taking *three hundred & eight* prisoners & two hundred & seventy five stand of arms."

Although not wounded at Gettysburg, in all Chamberlain would be wounded six times during the war. Later a brigade commander, he saw heavy action in the 1864 campaign against the Army of Northern Virginia. While leading his men in an attack against Petersburg he was seriously – indeed, it was believed mortally – wounded by a bullet that passed through his lower right abdomen. He was given a field promotion to brigadier-general; as Grant later described it, "Colonel J.L. Chamberlain, of the 20th Maine, was wounded on the 18th. He was gallantly leading his brigade at the time, as he had been in the habit of doing in all the engagements in which he had previously been engaged. He had several time been recommended for a brigadier-generalcy for gallant and meritorious conduct. On this occasion, however, I promoted him on the spot, and forwarded a copy of my order to the War Department, asking that my act might be confirmed and Chamberlain's name sent to the Senate for confirmation without any delay. This was done… ."

Despite continual pain from his wound, which never did heal completely, Chamberlain returned to the front in November 1864. At Five Forks (1 April 1865) he was breveted a major-general for his conduct; and a week later it was to Chamberlain that Gen. Grant gave the honor of receiving the formal surrender of the Army of Northern Virginia at Appomattox.

After the war he was offered a regular army commission, but declined it and was mustered out in January 1866. Returning to Maine, he was elected governor of the state, a post he won in two following elections. After leaving office in 1870 he returned to Bowdoin to become the college's president, also lecturing in political science and public law. He did maintain his military interests, however, serving as major-general of Maine's militia. He also had business interests in Florida, as well as serving as surveyor of the port of Portland, Maine; and he wrote about the war. He died at Portland in his 91st year, on 24 February 1919, as a long-delayed consequence of his Civil War wounds.

COUCH, Darius Nash (1832–97)

Darius Couch (**see Plate D2**) was born in Putnam County, New York, on 23 July 1832. A graduate of West Point in 1842, he was sent to the Mexican War with Company B, 4th US Artillery. There he took ill from severe intestinal dysentery which, coupled with the rheumatic fever from which he also appears to have suffered, virtually crippled him at various times throughout the rest of his life. Couch recovered in time to see his first action at Buena Vista (22–23 February 1847), of which he wrote that

This engraving of Darius Couch was made from a photograph taken when he was still a brigadier-general. Often ill following service in the far South as a young officer, he declined the chance to become commander of the Army of the Potomac during the Gettysburg campaign instead of Meade.

Couch was something of an intellectual; he had taken leave from the army after the Seminole War, pursuing field research into the flora and fauna of northern Mexico for the Smithsonian Institution, and in 1852 he discovered a species of platyfish which was named in his honor, *Xiphophorus couchiana*.

he saw "plenty signs of the battle. Wounded men who had crawled to a cover, horses likewise without their masters, stragglers behind bushes, etc, the dead and dying lying side by side. I nerved myself in the sight and looked on unmoved."

Breveted a first lieutenant for his gallant conduct in this battle, Couch subsequently saw service in the Seminole War (1849–50), for which he was commended by the Secretary of War. He resigned his commission in 1855 to marry, and joined a copper manufacturing business run by his father-in-law in Taunton, Massachusetts. This was a period when many dedicated officers despaired of a career in the tiny, cash-starved peacetime army, where promotion was desperately slow even for men of proven merit.

When the Civil War broke out, Couch was authorized by the state governor to raise the 7th Massachusetts Infantry, which he led to Washington in July 1861. He was quickly appointed a brigadier-general of volunteers and given a brigade command. When the Army of the Potomac began the Peninsula campaign (April–May 1862) he commanded the 1st Division, IV Corps. "It was a miserably fought affair," he wrote of his first battle in the campaign, at Williamsburg; "... a few thousand Confederates held us all in check seeing that our people went in by driblets." Couch's disillusionment with the army commander, George McClellan, deepened during the Seven Days, when he complained that "we commenced falling back at 11pm leaving many gallant men desperately wounded and in the enemy's hands... a perfect rout... the same soldiers that had fought so magnificently during the last seven days were now a mob."

Suffering from one of his recurrent bouts of illness, Couch offered to resign after these battles, but his resignation was not accepted and he went on sick leave. In September 1862 he was back in command of a division and, on 7 November 1862, of II Corps. He led his corps at Fredericksburg (13 December 1862), where he argued against Burnside's plan of attack. Subsequently the second in command of the army under Hooker, Couch found himself in effective command at Chancellorsville (1–6 May 1863) when the latter was stunned by the turn of events. Couch ably organized a defense, stabilizing the front after it had apparently fallen apart, and was twice wounded.

While he was on sick leave after Chancellorsville he met Lincoln, who offered him command of the Army of the Potomac, but he declined for health reasons, instead suggesting George Meade. Couch was then named to command the Department of the Susquehanna – right in the path of Lee's invasion of Pennsylvania, which was part of his department. Couch disagreed with state politicians during the campaign, and afterwards was sent to command the 2nd Division, XXIII Corps at Nashville, Tennessee, where he saw much action. The end of the war found him in North

George A. Custer rose from being a distinctly unpromising West Point cadet in the class of 1861, to brigadier-general of volunteers at the age of 23, to major-general's rank by the end of the war.

Carolina; resigning his commission on 9 June 1865, he returned home, where he ran unsuccessfully for governor of Massachusetts. After this defeat he moved to Connecticut, where he became the state's adjutant general. Couch died at Norwalk in February 1897.

CUSTER, George Armstrong (1839–76)

George Custer was born on 5 December 1839 in New Rumley, Ohio. While a teacher in Ohio he was appointed to West Point in 1857. Graduating last in his class of 1861, he was then assigned as a staff officer in the Army of the Potomac. He distinguished himself several times while holding the brevet rank of captain on the staffs of George B.McClellan and Alfred Pleasonton, and at the age of only 23 was appointed a brigadier-general of volunteers on 29 June 1863. He was assigned to command a brigade of Michigan cavalry in Judson Kilpatrick's division, first leading it at Gettysburg a few days later. Colonel J.H.Kidd, 6th Michigan Cavalry, later described the new brigadier:

"George A.Custer was, as all agree, the most picturesque figure of the civil war… Brave but not reckless; self-confident, yet modest; ambitious, but regulating his conduct at all times by a high sense of honor and duty; eager for laurels, but scorning to wear them unworthily; ready and willing to act… quick in emergencies, cool and self-possessed, his courage was of the highest moral type, his perceptions were intuitions… He was not a reckless commander. He was not regardless of human life… He was kind to his subordinates, tolerant of their weaknesses, always ready to help and encourage them. He was brave as a lion, fought as few men fought, but it was from no love of it."

Kidd also described his appearance: "An officer superbly mounted who sat his charger as if to the manor born. Tall, lithe, active, muscular, straight as an Indian and as quick in his movements, he had the fair complexion of a school girl. He was clad in a suit of black velvet, elaborately trimmed with gold lace, which ran down the outer seams of his trousers, and almost covered the sleeves of his cavalry jacket. The wide collar of a blue navy shirt was turned down over the collar of his velvet jacket, and a necktie of brilliant crimson was tied in a graceful knot at the throat, the long ends falling carelessly in front. The double rows of buttons on his breast were arranged in groups of twos, indicating the rank of brigadier-general. A soft, black hat with wide brim adorned with a gilt cord, and rosette encircling a silver star, was worn turned down on one side giving him a rakish air. His golden hair fell in

graceful luxuriance nearly or quite to his shoulders, and his upper lip was garnished with a blonde mustache. A sword and belt, gilt spurs and top boots completed his unique outfit." He further admitted that "Custer with flashing eye and flowing hair, charging at the head of his men, was a grand and picturesque figure, the more so by reason of his fantastic uniform, which made him a conspicuous mark for the enemy's bullets, but a coward in Custer's uniform would have become the laughing stock of the army."

Made a major-general of volunteers after Appomattox, he reverted to lieutenant-colonel on the regular army list after the war, assigned to the 7th Cavalry. Court-martialed for being absent without leave, and unwise in his public pronouncements, he was nevertheless restored to duty and took part in the 1867 campaign against the Sioux and Cheyenne; the Yellowstone Expedition of 1873; the expedition into the Black Hills in 1874; and the Cheyenne and Sioux campaign of 1876. It was during a detached march in this latter campaign that he divided his regiment in the face of a much larger Indian force at the Little Big Horn on 25 June 1876, in which action he and all the men under his personal command lost their lives.

FRANKLIN, William Buel (1823–1903)

William Franklin (**see Plate D3**) was born on 27 February 1823 at York, Pennsylvania. Ranked first in the West Point class of 1843 (in which U.S. Grant ranked 21st), he was commissioned into the Corps of Topographical Engineers. He took part in the Great Lakes survey and explorations in the Rocky Mountains. In the Mexican War he earned a brevet for bravery at Buena Vista.

From 1848 to 1852 he was an assistant professor at West Point; between 1852 and the Civil War he was in Washington, where he was in charge of building the Capitol dome and the monolithic Treasury addition. On the outbreak of the Civil War he was commissioned colonel of the 12th US Infantry, and shortly thereafter a brigadier-general of volunteers on 17 May 1861. He commanded a brigade at First Bull Run (21 July), and was given a divisional command that September. He served in this capacity in the Peninsula campaign (April–May 1862), during which he was given command of VI Corps. McClellan complained to his wife in August 1862 that Franklin showed "little energy", adding "I do not at all doubt Franklin's loyalty now, but his efficiency is very little – I am very sorry that it has turned out so. The main, perhaps the only cause is that he has been & still is sick – & one ought not to judge harshly a person in that condition."

Nevertheless, leading his corps with distinction, Franklin commanded the troops at Crampton's Gap at South Mountain (14 September 1862), and three days later fought at Antietam. Burnside picked him to command the Left Grand Division, consisting of I and VI Corps, at Fredericksburg that December. Franklin was bitter about Burnside's botched attack: "Both his staff and Smith's are talking outrageously, only repeating though, no doubt, the words of their generals," wrote Charles Wainwright after the battle. "Burnside may be unfit to command this army; his present plan may be absurd, and failure certain; but his lieutenants have no right to say so to their subordinates. As it is, Franklin has talked so much and so loudly to this effect ever since the present move was decided on, that he has completely demoralized his whole command, and so rendered failure doubly sure. His conduct has been such that he certainly deserves to be broken."

Burnside wanted Franklin removed from command, but Lincoln refused; instead he accepted Burnside's resignation. Marsena Patrick reported the rumor going through the army on 11 January 1863: "The contest is between Franklin & Hooker for the succession." Eventually, however, he had to record on 28 January that "Gen. Franklin was ordered to turn over the Command of the grand Division & report in Washington. Many persons think it is probable that Franklin will have a trial. Undoubtedly there is a great deal of disloyalty, according to Judge Holt's interpretation of that word, in Franklin's command."

William Buel Franklin as a major-general – a *Harper's Weekly* engraving after a Brady photograph. Academically one of the most distinguished of all Union general officers, he graduated top of his class at West Point and became a celebrated engineer. His high reputation saved his career when his outspoken criticism of superiors brought him into serious disfavor.

Franklin was not court-martialed; Capt. Charles Francis Adams Jr, 1st Massachusetts Cavalry, wrote that Franklin was "on the whole considered the ablest officer we have," and such a reputation may have saved him. However, he was not restored at once to a senior command. After some months he was given XIX Corps in the West, during both the Sabine Pass expedition and the Red River campaign (March–May 1864); he was wounded during the latter. At the end of the war Franklin was named president of the board for retiring disabled officers. However, his outspokenness against Burnside had so turned his fellow generals against him that he resigned his commission in 1866.

After the war Franklin served as vice-president and general manager of Colt's Fire Arms Manufacturing Co. until 1888. During that time he also supervised the building of the Connecticut state capitol, and was a Democratic presidential elector in the 1876 election. He was named commissioner general of the United States for the Paris Exposition in 1888. Returning to Connecticut, he died there on 8 March 1903, and is buried at York, Pennsylvania.

FRENCH, William Henry (1815–81)

William French was born on 13 January 1815 in Baltimore, Maryland. He was graduated with West Point's class of 1837, a classmate of John Sedgwick and Joseph Hooker, and assigned to the 1st US Artillery. He served in Florida and then in the Mexican War, where he was breveted a captain and a major for gallantry and meritorious conduct.

The outbreak of the Civil War found him in command of a garrison deep in Southern territory, at Eagle Pass, Texas. Rather than surrender to state authorities, he marched his men to the mouth of the Rio Grande and then embarked on boats to go to Key West, still under Federal authority. He was then appointed a brigadier-general of volunteers, ranking from 28 September 1861, and given a command in II Corps during the Peninsula campaign (April–May 1862). On 4 June 1862, Charles Haydon, an officer in the 2nd Michigan, recorded French being introduced to his command as a general "who greatly distinguished himself at Fair Oaks... He was cheered beyond measure. There is no doubt that he is one of the best fighting Generals in the army." With this reputation, French went on to be a division commander at Antietam that September, promoted to major-general on 29 November 1862. He continued in this command at Fredericksburg and Chancellorsville (December 1862 and May 1863), thereafter being transferred to command the District of Harper's Ferry.

After Chancellorsville, French succeeded to the command of III Corps. However, he was blamed for much of the failure of the Mine Run campaign in November 1863, especially by Meade. Marsena Patrick noted in his diary on 26 November that the army was delayed by the slowness of French's corps to move, adding, "Meade was very angry (& justly) at this terrible delay and carelessness... ." French was a stout and red-faced individual, and there was talk that his problems were caused by alcohol. He compounded his misfortune when his corps accidentally ran into the Confederates and brought on an engagement. "The blame for the failure is pretty generally laid upon General French," Charles Wainwright recorded on 29 November, adding on 10 December that the campaign's failure "was no doubt mainly owning to General French, who

I find it generally believed was drunk. I cannot vouch for the truth of this, however, and hope it was not so. He certainly lost his way twice, and appears to have acted very queerly."

French was aware of this muttering, and apparently fed misleading information to a correspondent with the *New York Herald*, which printed stories praising French's command. "It seems to be the idea," Patrick wrote on 6 December, "that this fellow is employed by French & his Clique, to forestall public opinion & set up French, before 'Official' papers are made public."

Perhaps these stories did their intended work. Indeed, there was even some talk that French, then senior corps commander in the Army of the Potomac, might be picked by the newly arriving U.S. Grant to replace Meade as army commander. This did not happen, however; French continued in his command until III Corps, much shrunken by the end of enlistments in the spring of 1864, was merged into another command. French was mustered out of volunteer service with effect from 6 May 1864. He served on various military boards until the end of the war, by which time he held the rank of colonel in command of the 4th US Artillery. He retired in 1880 and died in Washington on 20 May 1881, being buried in Rock Creek Cemetery.

GIBBON, John (1827–96)

Born in Philadelphia, Pennsylvania, on 20 April 1827, John Gibbon (**see Plate F3**) was graduated from the US Military Academy in 1847. He saw service in Mexico and in the Seminole War, and as an artillery instructor at West Point, writing a standard book on the subject thereafter. On the

George McClellan and Lincoln meet privately after Antietam in the fall of 1862. The president desperately wanted McClellan to resume the offensive, but the ever-cautious general continued to stall. When it was reported that the army's horses were worn out, Lincoln asked what on earth they'd done to *get* worn out?

When John Gibbon, a professional artilleryman, first earned command of an infantry brigade, contemporaries predicted that the unit would not be drilled in evolutions of the line, known only by infantry officers. Gibbon, however, bought and memorized a manual and astonished his peers with his well-drilled brigade. His command would become famous as the "Iron Brigade" of mid-Western troops, known by their Hardee hats – one of Gibbon's innovations to improve morale. At about the time of Gettysburg, the staff officer Frank Haskell described him as "compactly made, neither spare nor corpulent, with ruddy complexion, chestnut brown hair, with a clean-shaved face, except his moustache, which is decidedly reddish in color, medium-sized, well-shaped head, sharp, moderately-jutting brow, deep blue, calm eyes, sharp, slightly aquiline nose, compressed mouth, full jaws and chin, with an air of calm firmness in his manner. He always looks well dressed."

When this portrait was taken he was clearly in the early stages of growing what became a full beard.

outbreak of the Civil War he found himself – like so many other officers – in a difficult position; he had spent much of his youth in North Carolina, where his parents, who owned slaves, still lived, and his wife was from Baltimore, Maryland.

While he was serving at Camp Floyd, Utah, during the uncertain period between Lincoln's election and the Confederate firing on Fort Sumter, one evening the post band struck up *Dixie*, the Southern song, shortly after the band leader received a whispered message from Gibbon's small daughter. Some officers present at the incident wrote a letter to the Secretary of War claiming to uncover a pro-Southern plot and naming Gibbon as a Southern sympathizer. On learning this Gibbon wrote a heated letter to the Adjutant General denying these charges; he demanded a court-martial, which was convened on 5 July. After a one-day session Gibbon was cleared of charges. As a firm believer in the oath he had sworn to defend his country's Constitution and obey the officers of her army, rather than following the political agenda of any particular state, Gibbon was firmly in the Union camp.

He was named chief of artillery of Irvin McDowell's division until appointed a brigadier-general of volunteers on 2 May 1862. He was given command of the only brigade of troops from Western states, a hard-fighting unit that won the nickname of the "Iron Brigade". There he was described by one of his officers as "bland and genial," while another said he was "a plain, common man, [who] will listen to the complaint of a private as soon as he will to a colonel." Gibbon relied on incentives rather than punishment to maintain discipline. To improve morale he adopted the US Army's dress uniform, with added gaiters, for his brigade's field dress. On the other hand, no commander can ever be universally admired: one of his Wisconsin soldiers called him "a manufactured aristocrat, who owes all his importance to the circumstances that created him," adding that he was "arbitrary, severe and exacting… distant, formal and reserved."

In November 1862, Gibbon was given command of the 2nd Division, I Corps. Badly wounded at Fredericksburg (13 December 1862), he returned to duty after three months' recuperation. He was then placed in command of the 2nd Division of II Corps. In this appointment he was wounded once more at Gettysburg (1–3 July 1863).

After recovering again, Gibbon was given command of draft depots in Cleveland and Philadelphia. With the start of the 1864 campaign he returned to the Army of the Potomac, fighting with distinction at the head of his old division. He was promoted major-general ranking from 7 June 1864. In January 1865 he was given command of XXIV Corps in the Army of the James. He was one of the commissioners named to receive the surrender of the Army of Northern Virginia at Appomattox.

After the war Gibbon was named colonel on the regular army roster in command of the 36th US Infantry, transferring to the 7th US Infantry in 1869. He was involved in the 1876 campaign against the Sioux, followed by the Nez Perces campaign. He was named a brigadier-general in the regular army on 10 July 1885, and retired in 1891. Serving as commander in chief of the Military Order of the Loyal Legion, a veteran officers' organization, he died in Baltimore on 6 February 1896.

HANCOCK, Winfield Scott (1824–86)

Winfield Scott Hancock (see Plate F1) was born, one of twins, on 14 February 1824 near Norristown, Pennsylvania, where he is buried today. He was graduated towards the bottom of the West Point class of 1844, and was assigned to the infantry. He served in the Mexican War, winning a brevet for gallantry; in the Kansas War against the Seminoles; and in the Utah expedition. When the Civil War broke out he was chief quartermaster in the sleepy southern California town of Los Angeles. Returning east, he was immediately named a brigadier-general of volunteers, dating from 23 September 1861. As a brigade commander he served in the Army of the Potomac in the Peninsula campaign of April–May 1862.

It was on the Peninsula that he gained his nickname, when the army's commander telegraphed his wife with news of the day's battle, adding that "Hancock was superb". The dispatch found its way into print, and thereafter he was always "Hancock the Superb." The staff officer Frank Haskell afterwards wrote that Hancock was "the most magnificent looking General in the whole Army of the Potomac… the tallest and most shapely, and in many respects the best looking officer of them all. His hair is very light brown, straight and moist, and always looks well, his beard is of the same color, of which he wears the moustache and a tuft under the chin; complexion ruddy, features neither large nor small, but well cut, with full jaw and chin, compressed mouth, straight nose, full, deep blue eyes, and a very mobile, emotional countenance. He always dresses remarkably well, and his manner is dignified, gentlemanly and commanding. I think if he were in citizen's

Hancock, commander of II Corps, stands at left center with his hand on a tree. Francis Barlow, his jacket open to show a checked shirt, leans on the same tree; while John Gibbon is the third man to the right of Hancock, hatless, leaning on his sword, and wearing a single-breasted sack coat. Cf Plate F.

clothes, and should give commands in the army to those who did not know him, he would be likely to be obeyed at once, and without any question as to his right to command."

In September 1862 Hancock took his men into the Antietam campaign, and when Maj.Gen.Israel B.Richardson was mortally wounded he succeeded him in command of the 1st Division, II Corps; he formally received the rank of major-general of volunteers on 29 November 1862. He distinguished himself thereafter at Fredericksburg (December 1862), and after Chancellorsville (May 1863) his division covered the retreat of the Union army across the Rappahannock.

When he arrived on the field of Gettysburg on 1 July 1863 Hancock found I and XI Corps badly beaten, and immediately took command. He drew up a defensive line based on Cemetery Ridge, advising the army's new commander, Meade, to fight on this field rather than withdraw. Two days later, when the Confederates – led by such old friends of his as Lewis Armistead and Richard B.Garnett – struck his troops during Pickett's Charge, he was badly wounded when a bullet tore into his saddle, sending pieces of wood and a nail into his thigh. For a while his condition was cause for serious concern, but he recovered by the end of 1863 and was able to return to command II Corps.

Many of the senior figures in the Army of the Potomac were convinced that Hancock would succeed Meade as the army commander, but Grant retained Meade and kept Hancock as a corps commander. He led his corps in all the battles up to Petersburg in summer 1864, winning Grant's appreciation and promotion to the regular army rank of brigadier-general on 12 August. After the war Grant wrote:

"Hancock stands the most conspicuous figure of all the general officers who did not exercise a separate command. He commanded a corps longer than any other one, and his name was never mentioned as having committed in battle a blunder for which he was responsible. He was a man of very conspicuous personal appearance. Tall, well-formed and, at the time of which I now write, young and fresh-looking, he presented an appearance that would attract the attention of an army as he passed. His genial disposition made him friends, and his personal courage and his presence with his command in the thickest of the fight won for him the confidence of troops serving under him. No matter how hard the fight, [II Corps] always felt that their commander was looking after them."

When his Gettysburg wound reopened in November 1864 he was sent back to Washington to form a Veteran Reserve Corps, but this was only partially created. He was also given department command in February 1865, staying in that position until the end of the war. He was given command of the Department of the East in 1877, and while holding the appointment ran in the presidential election against James A.Garfield, who only narrowly beat him. Hancock died while still department commander on 9 February 1886.

HOOKER, Joseph (1814–79)

Joseph Hooker (**see Plate D1**) was born in Hadley, Massachusetts on 13 November 1814. After early education at Hopkins Academy in Hadley he went on to West Point, from where he was graduated in 1837. He served on various staffs during the Mexican War, winning brevets for all ranks up to that of lieutenant-colonel for his gallant and meritorious conduct. His permanent captaincy was given him in 1848, and he went on to serve as assistant adjutant general of the Pacific Division. Going on leave of absence in 1851, he resigned his commission in 1853 and took up farming near Sonoma, California.

Seeking a return to the army, Hooker was named a brigadier-general of volunteers in August 1861, and commanded a division of III Corps in the Peninsula campaign the following year. It was during this period that a newspaper headed one of its stories from the front, "Fighting – Joe Hooker"; thereafter he was known as "Fighting Joe Hooker", which he found embarrassing. He commanded his division and then I Corps in the Seven Days' Battles of June–July 1862, at Second Bull Run (Manassas) in August, and Antietam in September. At Fredericksburg that December he was given command of two corps as the Center Grand Division. His criticisms of Burnside during this campaign caused the latter to request his removal; but Lincoln chose to appoint him commander of the Army of the Potomac in Burnside's stead.

"Fighting Joe" Hooker – an accidental and, as it turned out, perhaps inappropriate nickname – had sandy hair and pale blue eyes. Hooker had a weakness for the ladies and his headquarters swarmed with them; as a result a certain class of women became known as "hookers", a term still in use today.

Hooker (front, second from right) with his staff. Whatever his failings in the field, he greatly improved morale in the Army of the Potomac after Fredericksburg with a combination of furloughs, dress parades, more clothes and equipment, and more food.

Colonel Charles Wainwright noted in his diary in May 1862 that "General Hooker has been of the pleasantest kind, and I have him a delightful man to serve with. I do not, however, like the way he has of always decrying the other generals of his own rank, whose every act he seems to find fault with." When Hooker was named army commander Wainwright went on to write: "His bravery is unquestioned, but he has not so far shown himself anything of a tactician, and at Williamsburg he certainly did not appear to be master of the situation. One great quality I think he has, a good judgment of men to serve under him. I am asked on all sides here if he drinks. Though thrown in very close contact with him through six months, I never saw him when I thought him the worse for liquor. Indeed, I should say that his failing was more in the way of women than whiskey." John Gibbon felt that "A great deal of his attractive frankness was assumed and he was essentially an intriguer. In his intrigues, he sacrificed his soldierly principles whenever such sacrifice could gain him political influence to further his own ends."

Hooker planned a flank move around Lee, moving west and crossing the Rappahannock, cutting rapidly through the Wilderness area, and hitting Lee where he would have to attack, between Fredericksburg and Richmond. Upon reaching the area, however, he apparently lost all resolve, and had his forces pull back to defensive lines around Chancellorsville. There Lee threw in a flank move of his own, and at dusk on 2 May 1863 Stonewall Jackson smashed through Hooker's right. Hooker's apparent paralysis of will persisted, and only the accidental death of Jackson, and hard fighting by Hooker's subordinates, saved the Union army from a worse disaster.

Relieved of command as Lee headed north into Pennsylvania two months later, Hooker was sent to the West with the ill-fated XI and XII Corps, later consolidated into XX Corps. There he fought quite well under command of U.S.Grant at Chattanooga in October 1863. After the war Grant wrote:

"Of Hooker I saw but little during the war. I had known him very well before, however. Where I did see him, at Chattanooga, his achievement in bringing his command around the point of Lookout Mountain and into Chattanooga Valley was brilliant. I nevertheless regarded him as a dangerous man. He was not subordinate to his superiors. He was ambitious to the extent of caring nothing for the rights of others. His disposition was, when engaged in battle, to get detached from the main body of the army and exercise a separate command, gathering to his standard all he could of his juniors."

After James McPherson was killed at Atlanta, Oliver O.Howard, who was subordinate to Hooker, was named to command the Army of Tennessee. Hooker, who held rank as a brigadier-general in the regular army and major-general of volunteers, asked to be relieved from "an army in which rank and service are ignored." Sherman let him go, and he only held a departmental command until he retired in 1868. He died in Garden City, New York, on 31 October 1879.

HUMPHREYS, Andrew Atkinson (1810–83)

Andrew Humphreys (see Plate H1) was born in Philadelphia on 2 November 1810, to a family of naval architects and constructors. After graduation from West Point in 1831 he was assigned to the Corps of Topographical Engineers, spending much of his time on hydrographical surveys of the Mississippi Delta until the Civil War broke out.

Assigned to the staff of George McClellan, commander of the Army of the Potomac, in 1861, Humphreys was named a brigadier-general of volunteers in April 1862. He served during the Peninsula campaign as the army's chief topographical engineer, a post well fitted for his methodical and precise character. In September 1862 he was given command of a newly recruited division in V Corps, which he quickly brought to a high state of combat readiness. Colonel Charles Wainwright noted at Fredericksburg that December that "Humphreys's division of entirely new troops quite rivaled the old Second Corps." He led them with distinction in the Antietam campaign, at Fredericksburg in December, and at Chancellorsville in May 1863, where he proved himself to be iron-willed and always cool in action.

Given command of a division in III Corps, Humphreys held off attacks at Gettysburg (1–3 July 1863) by superior Confederate forces. For this action he was named a major-general of volunteers, as well as a brevet brigadier-general in the regular army. General Meade asked him to become chief of staff of the Army of the Potomac, in which appointment he served until November 1864. The initial announcement came as a surprise to many; Marsena Patrick noted in his diary on 9 July, "Gen. Humphreys was announced as Chief of Staff, to the surprise of all, as it has been understood that Gen. Warren would have that position." Patrick did not think much of Humphreys' suitability; however, his service met with the approval of Meade and, later, of Grant.

Andrew Atkinson Humphreys photographed in the field when he was still serving as chief topographical engineer of the Army of the Potomac. He was one of the few officers who made a successful transition from staff to field command.

When Winfield Hancock's ill health forced him to give up his command in November 1864, Grant picked Humphreys to take over the veteran but worn-down II Corps. Grant's aide, Horace Porter, reflected headquarters thinking when he wrote, "His appointment was recognized as eminently fitting, and met with favor throughout the entire army"; but this was not wholly true. John Gibbon, the senior divisional commander in the corps, took great exception to being passed over. He asked to be relieved, while assuring Humphreys that he was doing so not out of a refusal to serve under him but because he felt he was being slighted. As to Humphreys, Gibbon said, the general was "one of the most accomplished soldiers and highest-toned gentlemen in the army." Luckily for the army, Grant declined to give in to Gibbon, whom he retained in command of his division.

Humphreys did an excellent job in revitalizing the II Corps, leading it in all operations up to Appomattox. He was given the rank of brevet major-general in the regular army for his gallantry at Sailor's Creek. After the war, in August 1866 he was named a brigadier-general in the regular army, with the post of chief of engineers. He served in this position until he retired in 1879. He also produced an excellent account entitled *The Virginia Campaign of 1864–65*. He died in Washington, DC on 27 December 1883.

HUNT, Henry Jackson (1819–89)

Henry Hunt (**see Plate C3**) was born in Detroit on 14 September 1819. A third-generation regular army officer, Hunt was graduated from West Point in 1839. He served as a lieutenant of artillery in Winfield Scott's audacious advance on Mexico City in August 1847, earning brevets to captain and major for gallantry. At Churubusco he galloped his gun up to the walls of the capital; as the gun unlimbered almost every man and horse was hit, but the survivors got the piece into position only yards from a Mexican gun. Both crews were loading with desperate haste, but in the end it was Hunt's gun that fired first. After the Mexican War, Hunt was named to a board of three artillerymen who were to revise the system of light artillery tactics then in use. Their manual was adopted by the army in 1860 and became the standard system for both sides in the Civil War.

Hunt served at First Bull Run (Manassas – 21 July 1861) and was then named chief of artillery for the Washington defenses; he was also given responsibility for training the artillery reserve of the Army of the Potomac. Hunt pioneered massed artillery use in the Union army, assembling at Malvern Hill (1 July 1862) some 100 guns, which almost alone broke up the Confederate attacks. He served with distinction at Antietam (17 September 1862), being named a brigadier-general of volunteers two days before the battle.

Although a regular army man, and known for dressing down battery commanders for wasting expensive ammunition, Hunt was informal with his staff. Provost Marshal Marsena Patrick, himself somewhat stiff-necked, noted in his diary on 31 December 1862 – New Year's Eve – that he went to bed at a quarter of ten, "but was again roused by the Card players at Hunt['s] Tent – I remained awake an hour, then wrote a note & sent it, a little after 12 o'clock, requesting the noise to be stopped."

At Gettysburg (1–3 July 1863) Hunt placed 77 guns along the Union front, withdrawing several batteries there during the counter-battery fight with the Confederate guns given the job of softening up the Union center for Pickett's Charge. He got them back, with enough ammunition for the job, in time to help stop the attack; and was breveted major-general of volunteers for his service. However, Hunt, a Democrat, stayed in contact with George McClellan, who ran for president against Lincoln; and in September 1864 Hunt wrote to McClellan that an armistice with the South could lead to peace, and the Democratic Party platform was aimed at the South "to detach the people from their leaders," and should be supported by McClellan.

In June 1864, Ulysses S.Grant placed Hunt in charge of all siege operations at Petersburg. At the end of the war he was named a major-general in the regular army, but reverted to his permanent rank of

Henry Hunt, the brilliant and highly successful Army of the Potomac artillery commander, with Maj. James Duane, the army's chief engineer, in the lines at Petersburg, as shown in an engraving in the 15 October 1864 issue of *Harper's Weekly*. In March 1865 a subordinate, Col. Charles Wainwright, recalled a ride along Union lines in Hunt's company: "The General was in the most excellent spirits, and amused me very much as well as filling me with wonder at his memory... quoting page after page; and then almost whole volumes of comic poetry, interspersed with stories. Still he saw everything as we rode along and was just as much alive to the object of his visit to the lines as if he had been thinking and talking of nothing else. He is certainly one of the most wonderful men I have ever met. With a very retentive memory, he is always forgetting; most original and practical in all his ideas, he is most impractical in carrying them out... ." Nevertheless, Hunt had shown heroism and energy as a young officer of the "flying artillery" in the Mexican War.

lieutenant-colonel in the 3rd US Artillery. He was named colonel commanding the 5th US Artillery in 1869, serving until he retired in 1883. He was appointed governor of the Soldiers' Home in Washington in 1885, dying there on 11 February 1889.

KEARNY, Philip (1815–62)

Philip Kearny was born in New York City on 2 June 1815. The scion of a wealthy, socially prominent family, he was graduated from Columbia University in 1833. He inherited a million dollars in 1836 – an almost unimaginable sum at that date – but nevertheless decided to follow his dream into the army. Commissioned into his uncle's regiment, the 1st Dragoons, in 1837 as a second lieutenant, Kearny attended the French cavalry school at Saumur in 1839. He served with the Chasseurs d'Afrique in Algiers in 1840, returning to serve on the staff of the Major-General Commanding the Army.

On Winfield Scott's staff in Mexico, at Churubusco (20 August 1847) Kearny was badly wounded in the left arm, which was subsequently amputated. Recovering, he then served in California until he resigned in 1851. He then traveled the world before retiring to his New Jersey estate. In 1859 he went to Europe to join the French Imperial Guard in the Italian campaign of that year, serving at Solferino and Magenta.

On the outbreak of the Civil War, Kearny returned to the army and was quickly appointed a brigadier-general of volunteers in command of a New Jersey brigade. He was made a major-general on 4 July 1862, commanding a division in III Corps in the Peninsula campaign. Proud of his own men, he once addressed some stragglers only to find that they were from a different command. To ensure that this never happened again, on 27 June 1862 he issued the following order: "The general commanding division directs that officers in command of companies are to wear a piece of red flannel two inches square on the front of their caps. Field officers to wear the same upon the top of the cap – this to be done immediately that they may be recognized in action." After Kearny's death the practice was ordered continued, and enlisted men also began wearing these "Kearny's patches". This was the origin of what would become an army-wide system of divisional identification after Hooker took over.

The extraordinary Philip Kearny – an engraving in *Harper's Weekly* of 20 September 1862, after a Brady photograph. According to the paper, "General McClellan is said to have wept when he heard of his death, and to have said: 'Who can replace Phil Kearney?' ". The inheritor of enormous wealth, this hero of the battle of Churubusco (1847) still pursued the profession of arms so hungrily that when US Army service palled he traveled to serve with the French army in North Africa and Italy. Note that the engraving process has reversed the portrait left for right – it was Kearny's left arm that he lost in Mexico, and his coat is shown here buttoning the female way.

Kearny was unhappy with what he perceived as timidity among the Union senior commanders. After the Peninsula campaign had stalled Charles Wainwright confided to his diary, "[Kearny] is full of the possibility of our capturing Richmond at this time; says he could do it with his division, and that two or three divisions could do it easily. He talked very wild, as usual. Still, there may be something in what he says."

Kearny would never have the chance to be tested at any higher level of command than a division. At Chantilly, on 1 September 1862, in a heavy rain storm, he rode by accident into Confederate lines. Called on to surrender, he spurred his horse instead and, while trying to escape, was shot and killed. Lee himself sent a message through the lines reporting Kearny's death, and his body was turned over to Union authorities to be returned to his family. He was originally buried at Trinity Church, New York City, but in 1912 was reburied in Arlington National Cemetary.

Colonel David Strother noted in his diary on 2 September 1862: "Heard the news that General Kearny had been killed last night and his body sent in by the enemy under a flag. Thus ends the one-armed hero of the war, a man of great valor and energy and a serious loss for us." This was the general opinion of the army.

McCLELLAN, George Brinton (1826–85)

George McClellan (**see Plate C1**) was born in Philadelphia on 3 December 1826. Attending the University of Pennsylvania, he left in order to enter West Point, where he was graduated second in his class of

1846. Appointed to the Corps of Engineers, he was noted for getting roads and bridges built during Scott's Mexico City campaign of 1847, earning two brevets. Thereafter he returned to West Point as an instructor; translated a French bayonet manual; explored the sources of the Red River; was one of a group of US Army observers during the Crimean War; designed a saddle for army use that was based on the Hungarian model; and surveyed possible transcontinental railroad routes. He resigned his commission as captain, 1st Cavalry, in 1857 to become chief engineer of the Illinois Central Railroad.

At the outbreak of the Civil War he was president of the Ohio & Mississippi Railroad; he volunteered his services to Ohio's governor, who on 23 April 1861 appointed McClellan a major-general to organize the state forces. So well did he perform this task that President Lincoln appointed him a major-general in the regular army – as its second ranking officer – in June 1861.

McClellan was successful in West Virginia in June and July – a time of few successes – and Lincoln brought him East to command the Army of the Potomac in August, naming him General-in-Chief of the Armies of the United States on 1 November 1861 in succession to Winfield Scott. He set about rebuilding the army's morale, getting clothes and food for the troops, while holding parade after parade to instil pride and confidence. McClellan himself did not lack for confidence, writing on 21 May 1862, "When I see the hand of God guarding one so weak as myself, I can almost think myself a chosen instrument to carry out his schemes."

Blessed with a versatile mind and sweeping interests, George McClellan made a technically perfect commander for the Army of the Potomac, in which appointment his handsome looks and gentlemanly manners also earned him many admirers. However, his unshakable self-confidence was allied to excessive caution, and a total lack of political instinct; and when his lack of nerve in combat situations led to repeated failure in 1862, Lincoln dismissed him. That this came as a complete surprise to him says much about McClellan's limitations.

In March 1862, President Lincoln, frustrated by McClellan's inactivity, relieved him of his generalship-in-chief to concentrate on his army command and gave him a direct order to take the field. McClellan finally shipped his Army of the Potomac to the Peninsula that juts into Chesapeake Bay, planning a rapid march to take Richmond. Faulty intelligence, which he believed despite evidence to the contrary, indicated that Confederate forces greatly out-numbered him. After making laborious preparations to conduct a siege at Yorktown that never happened, the Union army almost reached Richmond, only to be attacked by the Confederates under Joseph Johnston (Fair Oaks, 31 May–1 June), and then again under Robert E.Lee (Gaine's Mill, 27 June). McClellan, thoroughly unnerved by these attacks, rejected the advice of Kearny and Hooker that Richmond was still vulnerable, and withdrew to a defendable base on the James River.

He was then ordered to bring the army back to northern Virginia to support John Pope's abortive campaign, which failed at

Second Bull Run (Manassas – 30 August). As Lee headed into Maryland, McClellan followed, and even had the luck to obtain a copy of Lee's battle plan. Moving rapidly – for McClellan – he struck Lee's divided army at Antietam (17 September). The Union attacks were piecemeal, however, and Lee's greatly outnumbered forces held, inflicting great losses; two days later they withdrew across the Potomac, unmolested.

McClellan followed Lee with characteristic caution. Lincoln visited his headquarters; but unable to persuade him to act aggressively, the President dismissed McClellan from command of the Army of the Potomac and replaced him with Ambrose Burnside on 7 November 1862. Most of the army were as shocked as was McClellan. "The greatest indignation is expressed by everyone here, even those who have blamed McClellan [for the army's failure to succeed]," Charles Wainwright wrote in his dairy the next day. On the 9th he noted that some officers, on McClellan's farewell, used "expressions with regret to his removal which they had no right to use, and a few even going so far as to beg him to resist the order, and saying that the army would support him." Even a private in the 9th New York, Edward Wightman, wrote home that "there seems to be a general impression that this is no time to change field officers… ."

McClellan was unusual among general officers in nearly always being photographed wearing his buff sash; he was also known for being accompanied by a large staff when in the field. This photograph was taken in the fall of 1861.

McClellan went home to Trenton, New Jersey, fully expecting orders to resume his command; but they never came. The Democratic Party nominated this conservative to run against Lincoln in the 1864 presidential election on a peace platform. He duly resigned his commission on election day; but his bid failed, in part due to Lincoln's overwhelming support from soldiers who voted in the field. McClellan later became governor of New Jersey; he died on 19 October 1885 at Orange, New Jersey, and was buried in Riverview Cemetery, Trenton.

In 1866 William Swinton, who had been a reporter for the *New York Times* during the war, wrote a history of the army, which he had accompanied. Of McClellan he wrote: "He was assuredly not a great general; for he had the pedantry of war rather than the inspiration of war. His talent was eminently that of the cabinet; and his proper place was in Washington, where he should have remained as general-in-chief. Here his ability to plan campaigns and form large strategic combinations, which was remarkable, would have had full scope; and he would have been considerate and helpful to those in the field. But his power as a tactician was much inferior to his talent as a strategist, and he executed less boldly than he conceived: not appearing to know well those counters with which a commander must work – time, place, and circumstance."

McDOWELL, Irvin (1818–85)

Irvin McDowell (see Plate A3) was born in Columbus, Ohio, on 15 October 1818. At first educated in France, he was graduated in the US

Military Academy class of 1838, and taught tactics at the Academy from 1841 to 1845. He served as a staff officer in the Mexican War, earning a captain's brevet for gallantry at Buena Vista (22 February 1847). From then until the outbreak of the Civil War he was assigned to duty in the office of the Adjutant General of the Army.

On 14 May 1861 he was appointed a brigadier-general in the regular army, although he had exercised no command until that point. He was given command of the Army of the Potomac and directed to lead it on Richmond. McDowell believed that the army was unready to take the field, and later testified to Congress: "There was not a man there who had ever manoeuvred troops in large bodies. There was not one in the army; I did not believe there was one in the whole country; at least, I knew there was no one there who had ever handled 30,000 troops. I had seen them handled abroad in reviews and marched, but I have never handled that number, and no one here had. I wanted very much a little time; all of us wanted it. We did not have a bit of it. The answer was: 'You are green, it is true; but they are green, also; you are all green alike'."

His campaign plan was a good one, but his ill-trained force fell apart at First Bull Run (Manassas) on 21 July, and he was replaced in command of the army by George McClellan. In March 1862 he was named a major-general of volunteers and given command of a corps in the Army of the Potomac. His corps was left to defend Washington during the Peninsula campaign, but took the field in the Second Bull Run campaign in summer 1862.

Colonel David Strother met McDowell in June 1862 and noted in his diary: "His manner is not strong but his conversation was clear and concise, showing a good understanding of the subject in hand." A month later he had a chance to talk further with McDowell: "Sitting down, we had a very pleasant half of an hour [talking] chiefly about trouting, of which he is very fond. His manners are very kind and he talks agreeably... ."

McDowell was blamed for the army's defeat in the Second Bull Run campaign almost as much as was John Pope, its commander. It had not helped him that many of his troops, at all levels, basically distrusted his loyalty to the Union. McDowell himself complained to Marsena Patrick on 12 July 1862 "that [Brig.Gen. Abner] Doubleday has been the cause of more evil to him than any one else, having made the matter of his guarding rebel property the test of his loyalty".

McDowell was relieved from command and spent two years of inactivity, finally being assigned as commander of the Department of the Pacific on 1 July 1864. He later commanded both the Department of the East and that of the South before returning to command the Department of the Pacific. He died in San Francisco on 4 May 1885, and is buried at the Presidio there.

Irvin McDowell had the ill fortune to be the first commander of the wholly unprepared Army of the Potomac in its unsuccessful First Bull Run (Manassas) campaign of July 1861. He had previously been involved with construction projects in Washington, DC, as a professional engineer, and as a long-time staff officer he had very little experience of command. He was perfectly well aware of his own and his army's failings, but was unjustly blamed for the outcome when the government forced him into premature action.

MEADE, George Gordon (1815–72)

George Meade (**see Plate E1**) was born in Cadiz, Spain, on 31 December 1815, the son of a wealthy American merchant who was wiped out financially by adhering to Spain's cause in the Napoleonic Wars. Returning to the United States, Meade attended Mount Hope Institution and then the US Military Academy, from which he was graduated in 1835. He saw service in Florida and at the Watertown Arsenal before resigning in 1836 to work as a civil engineer. He returned to the army on 19 May 1842 as a second lieutenant in the Corps of Topographical Engineers, thereafter working mostly on building lighthouses and breakwaters and doing coastal and geodetic survey work. He saw action in the Mexican War, being breveted a first lieutenant.

At the outbreak of the Civil War, Capt. Meade was made a brigadier-general of volunteers and given command of a Pennsylvania brigade, which he led in the Peninsula campaign. He was badly wounded at Glendale (30 June 1862), one of the defensive battles fought by dispersed Union corps as they retreated to the James River. Recovering in time for Second Bull Run (Manassas), he was given command of a division in I Corps at Fredericksburg (13 December 1862); shortly thereafter he was given V Corps. He was named to replace Joseph Hooker as commander of the Army of the Potomac on 28 June 1863, just three days before Gettysburg. The army's fifth commander in just ten months, his personal contribution to the Union's great victory in that battle has always been a matter for discussion, and he was criticized for failing to pursue the retreating Confederates vigorously. Marsena Patrick noted in his diary on 16 November 1863 that Meade was "profoundly ignorant of the wants & necessities of the Army," adding that he would probably "never learn."

Staff officer Frank Haskell described Meade as "a tall spare man, with full beard, which with his hair, originally brown, is quite thickly sprinkled with gray – has a romanish face, very large nose, and a white, large forehead, prominent and wide over the eyes, which are full and large, and quick in their movements, and he wears spectacles. His *fibres* are all of the long and sinewy kind. His habitual personal appearance is quite careless, and it would be difficult to make him look well dressed."

Meade was terribly short-tempered. While leading a column of prisoners to the rear during the fighting in the Wilderness, Patrick noted in his diary that he "met Meade, who was in a terrible stew & declared that I was on the wrong road & going directly into the enemy's lines – I soon cooled him off however & in a huff was told to 'Go my own way', which I did, keeping the prisoners on the road they started, all right."

Although Lincoln was unhappy that Lee was allowed to escape from Gettysburg, Meade retained his army command right through to Appomattox. He was named a brigadier-general

George Gordon Meade as a major-general. Meade thought that he would be replaced as commander of the Army of the Potomac after earning Lincoln's displeasure for his failure to destroy Lee's army after Gettysburg, at Bristoe Station, and at Mine Run; but he was retained in command until the end of the war. He looks lugubrious in portraits, but was known for his hot temper: a contemporary called him a "damned old goggle eyed snapping turtle."

George Meade, standing center right foreground, facing left; the general in the bowler-type hat and open-necked coat standing behind Meade at right is John Sedgwick. They are seen here with their staffs at their headquarters in Falmouth, Virginia, in late 1863.

in the regular army on 7 July 1863, and a major-general late in the war. He held commands of various departments after the war, eventually being in charge of the Division of the Atlantic. He died at his headquarters in Philadelphia on 6 November 1872, and is buried in Laurel Hill Cemetery there. After the war, Grant wrote:

"General Meade was an officer of great merit, with drawbacks to his usefulness that were beyond his control. He had been an officer of the engineer corps before the war, and consequently had never served with troops until he was over forty-six years of age. He never had, I believe, a command of less than a brigade. He saw clearly and distinctly the position of the enemy, and the topography of the country in front of his own position. His first idea was to take advantage of the lay of the ground, sometimes without reference to the direction we wanted to move afterwards. He was subordinate to his superiors in rank to the extent that he could execute an order which changed his own plans with the same zeal he would have displayed if the plan had been his own. He was brave and conscientious, and commanded the respect of all who knew him. He was unfortunately of a temper that would get beyond his control, at times, and make him speak to officers of high rank in the most offensive manner. No one saw this fault more plainly than he himself, and no one regretted it more. This made it unpleasant at times, even in battle, for those around him to approach him even with information."

(continued on page 41)

MAY 1861
1: Major-General Commanding the Army
   Winfield Scott
2: Major-General Benjamin Butler
3: Brigadier-General Irvin McDowell

A

AUGUST 1862
1: Major-General John Pope
2: Major-General Fitz John Porter
3: Major-General Edwin Sumner

B

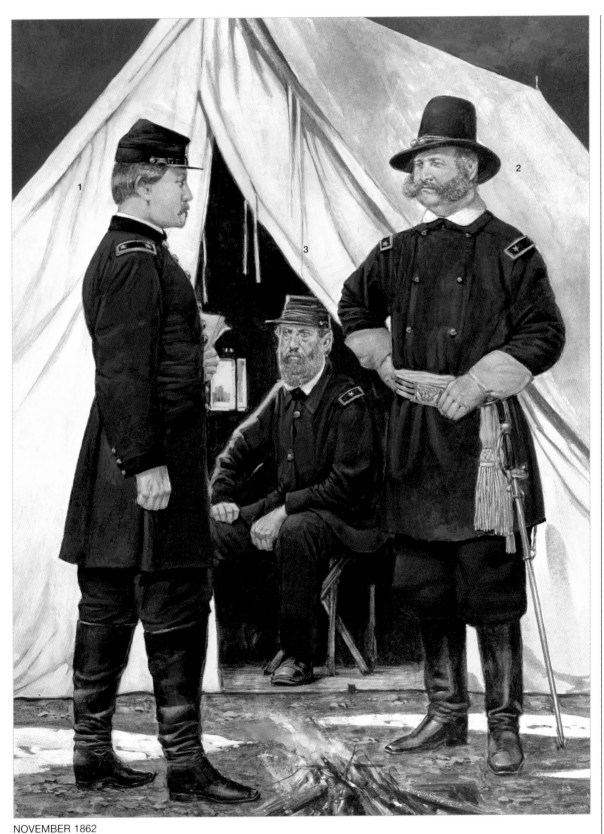

NOVEMBER 1862
1: Major-General George McClellan   2: Major-General Ambrose Burnside   3: Brigadier-General Henry Hunt

C

MAY 1863
1: Major-General Joseph Hooker   2: Major-General Darius Couch   3: Major-General William Franklin

D

JUNE 1863
1: Major-General George Meade
2: Major-General John Reynolds
3: Major-General Daniel Sickles

E

II CORPS COMMANDERS, AUTUMN 1864
1: Major-General Winfield Scott Hancock
2: Brigadier-General Francis Barlow
3: Brigadier-General John Gibbon

F

CAVALRY COMMANDERS OF THE ARMY OF THE POTOMAC
1: Brigadier-General George Stoneman   2: Major-General Alfred Pleasonton   3: Major-General Philip Sheridan

G

PETERSBURG, MAY 1864
1: Major-General Andrew Humphreys
2: Major-General John Sedgwick
3: Major-General Joshua Chamberlain

H

PLEASONTON, Alfred (1824–97)

Alfred Pleasonton (**see Plate G2**) was born in Washington, DC on 7 July 1824. Graduated in the West Point class of 1844, he was assigned to the dragoons. He earned a first lieutenant's brevet for gallantry in the Mexican War, and also served in Florida and on the frontier. He gained staff experience as an adjutant under Gen. William S.Harney. In 1861 he was a captain in the 2nd Dragoons (redesignated the 2nd Cavalry), and commanded the regiment as it marched from Utah to Washington that fall.

Promoted major on 15 February 1862, Pleasonton distinguished himself in the Peninsula campaign, and was made a brigadier-general of volunteers on 18 July 1862. He was given command of a cavalry division in the Antietam campaign, leading it at Fredericksburg (13 December 1862) and Chancellorsville (1–6 May 1863). He was given command of the Cavalry Corps of the Army of the Potomac on 7 June 1863, with promotion to major-general on 22 June.

Pleasonton was regarded with some suspicion by his peers. Colonel Charles R.Lowell, 2nd Massachusetts, said of him: "I can't call any cavalry officer good who can't see the truth and tell the truth. With an infantry officer this is not so essential, but cavalry are the eyes and ears of the army and ought to see and hear and tell truly; and yet it is the universal opinion that P's own reputation and P's late promotions are bolstered up by systematic lying." Captain Charles Francis Adams Jr, 1st Massachusetts, wrote to his mother that "Pleasonton is the bete noire of all cavalry officers… He is pure and simple a newspaper humbug. You always see his name in the papers, but to us who have served under him he is notorious as a bully and a toady… Yet mean and contemptible as Pleasonton is, he is always *in* at Head Quarters."

Brig.Gen. Alfred Pleasonton wears a typical field uniform of a sack coat and a broad-brimmed hat in this photograph taken in April 1863.

However, Pleasonton was well respected by at least some of the army's commanders. In a letter to his wife on 18 August 1862, McClellan said: "I am glad to inform you that your friend Pleasonton has done *splendidly*. I placed him in command of the rear guard. The little fellow [Pleasonton] brightened up very much this morning when he came to report. I looked very sternly at him & told him that I had a very serious complaint to make against him. He looked rather wild, injured, & disgusted & wished to know what it was. I replied that he had entirely disappointed me, that he had not created a single stampede, nor called for any reinforcements. That such heinous conduct was something I did not at all look for, & that if it was persisted in, I must send him to Pope. The little fellow began to grin & was well pleased. He *is* a most excellent soldier & has performed a very important duty most admirably."

Pleasonton led the cavalry in its first successful large operation of the war, surprising J.E.B.Stuart at Brandy Station (9 June 1863), in which action the Union cavalry was said to have come of age. However, his work in the Gettysburg campaign

was lackluster. He disapproved of the "Kilpatrick-Dahlgren Raid" against Richmond in February 1864, something that Grant thought was a good idea. As Grant had in mind for Philip Sheridan to command the cavalry in the East, this disagreement was the spur for Pleasonton's relief from command and reassignment to the Department of the Missouri.

There he performed well enough against the Confederate "Missouri Raid" in October 1864. Breveted major-general at the end of the war, he still reverted to his regular rank of major, 2nd US Cavalry. In 1866 Pleasonton was offered a lieutenant-colonelcy in the 20th US Infantry, but declined it. Since this resulted in his being subordinate to Col. T.J.H.Wood, who had graduated from West Point a year after Pleasonton and was lower on the list of volunteer major-generals, and to Lt.Col. I.N.Palmer, who graduated two years after Pleasonton and had only been breveted major-general, Pleasonton resigned. Although he applied for retirement at his volunteer rank, this was refused. He held some minor Federal posts, but in 1888 he was placed on the retired list as a major. He died in Washington on 17 February 1897, and is buried in the Congressional Cemetery there.

POPE, John (1822–92)

John Pope (see Plate B1) was born into a distinguished family in Louisville, Kentucky, on 16 March 1822. After graduating from West Point in 1842, he was twice breveted in the Mexican War. Commissioned a captain in the Corps of Topographical Engineers in 1856, he was named a brigadier-general of volunteers on 14 June 1861.

Pope led the forces that opened the upper Mississippi River just above Memphis, capturing Madrid and Island No.10. Promoted to major-general on 22 March 1862, he commanded the left wing of the army that besieged Corinth, Mississippi. Because of these successes he was called to Washington to command a new Army of Virginia, made up of troops around Washington and in the Shenandoah Valley.

Colonel David Strother met Pope in June 1862, and described him in his diary: "He is a stout man of medium height, prepossessing manners and appearance. He is young and alert… ." Later he added: "He reads character and talks like a keen, cool man of the world, kindly withal… Pope is a much cleverer man than I took him for." Two months later Strother wrote: "Pope is a bright, dashing man, self-confident and clearheaded. He has a good memory and has been a topographical engineer. I observe that he is wonderfully quick to seize all information on this subject. He remembers it all if once told and wants new details. Whether his mind grasps general subjects with capacity and clearness I have not had an opportunity to judge. He is irascible and impulsive in his judgments of men, but in his pleasant moods, jolly, humorous, and clever in conversation."

Named a brigadier-general in the regular army with effect from 14 July 1862, Pope issued a series of orders, the first telling his new command, "I have come to you from the West, where we have always seen the backs of our enemies… ." Having irritated his own troops, he made the enemy even madder by calling for his troops to live off the resources of Virginia's citizens, and authorizing them to inflict capital punishment on any guerrillas who had sworn an oath of allegiance to the USA and were later captured in arms against the government. Lee determined to decisively beat Pope's army, which he did in the Second Bull Run (Manassas) campaign of August 1862. Many of Pope's own generals were highly critical of him, both before and after Second Manassas.

Pope's army was afterwards merged into the Army of the Potomac, and he was sent to command the Department of the Northwest. He served well there during the Sioux uprising in Minnesota in 1863. Staying in the army after the war, he became a major-general on 26 October 1882 and held various departmental commands until his retirement in 1886. He died in Sandusky,

Fitz John Porter was tall, striking, a perfect-looking soldier, but lacked the political instincts needed to survive. He foolishly committed to paper criticisms of his superior officer, John Pope, which would come back to haunt him.

Ohio, on 23 September 1892, and is buried in Bellefontaine Cemetery, St Louis.

PORTER, Fitz John (1822–1901)

Fitz John Porter (**see Plate B2**) was born in Portsmouth, New Hampshire, to a naval family that included Commodore David Porter and Rear Admiral David Dixon Porter. He attended Exeter and was appointed to West Point, graduating in 1845. He was assigned to the artillery, and during the Mexican War he was wounded in the attack on Mexico City and received two brevets for gallantry. After the war he was assigned as an assistant artillery instructor at West Point until 1855. He was then adjutant of the command sent to Utah in 1857, serving there until 1860.

At the outbreak of the Civil War he was made colonel of the 15th US Infantry, as well as a brigadier-general of volunteers ranking from 17 May 1861. He served as chief of staff under Gen. Robert Patterson in the Shenandoah Valley during the First Bull Run campaign, before being recalled to help George McClellan whip the new Army of the Potomac into shape.

Porter commanded a division of III Corps at the outset of the Peninsula campaign, moving up to command of V Corps during the Seven Days' Battles. He displayed outstanding leadership in extricating his corps from constant attacks by superior Confederate forces, withdrawing to Malvern Hill, where he oversaw a huge defeat of the attacking Confederates (1 July 1862). For this action he was promoted to major-general of volunteers, as well as receiving a brevet to brigadier-general in the regular army.

When McClellan's army was withdrawn from the Peninsula to aid Pope's army in northern Virginia, Porter was ordered to come to Pope's aid; but *New York Times* reporter William Swinton, who covered the Army of the Potomac, wrote that "the order which Pope sent at half-past four, did not reach Porter till about dusk. He then made dispositions for attack, but it was too late. It is, however, more than doubtful that even had the order been received in time, any thing but repulse would have resulted from its execution."

Afterwards, Porter, who despised Pope, was discovered to have written about the latter in insubordinate terms. Knowing how close Porter was to McClellan, Pope, unable to have McClellan himself court-martialed, instead charged Porter with disloyalty, disobedience and misconduct in the face of the enemy. Porter, who advised McClellan not to commit his V Corps to a final attack at Antietam (17 September 1862), and hence allowed Lee to escape total defeat, was relieved from command after McClellan's own relief left him unprotected. He was tried by a military commission. Charles Wainwright, a McClellan supporter who suspected that the actual reason was the friendship between McClellan and Porter, added: "On the whole I cannot say that I am sorry, for I think I shall like Reynolds quite as much, and have a great deal more respect from him."

The commission found Porter guilty, and on 21 January 1863 ordered him "forever disqualified from holding any office of trust or profit under the Government of the United States." Wainwright felt that "From the manner of getting up the charges and of the formation of the court, I made up my mind at once that the case was to go against him. It was necessary for the Administration that it should: some scapegoat had to be found for the shortcomings of their pet, Pope, and in Porter they could hit a friend of McClellan at the same time. He may have been guilty of everything charged against him, or he may have been perfectly innocent, of this I know nothing; his condemnation was a foregone conclusion."

Porter spent the next 16 years seeking reinstatement to the US Army. Finally, a board headed by Gen. John M.Schofield exonerated Porter on 19 March 1879, and recommended his reinstatement. The current president, Republican Rutherford B.Hayes – who had actually lost the election but obtained office through political maneuvering – declined to act on the board's findings. Finally, on 4 May 1882, President Chester Arthur – a Democrat on the opposite side of the political fence from Hayes – ordered a full remission of the findings of the Porter court-martial, restoring his rank as a colonel of infantry from 14 May 1861. Porter died in Morristown, New Jersey, on 21 May 1901, and was buried in Green-Wood Cemetery, Brooklyn, New York.

Porter (seated, center) and his staff at his headquarters, photographed not long after the battle of Gaines' Mill (27 June 1862), where Porter had managed to extract his corps from heavy Confederate assaults. A close associate of McClellan, Porter fell when McClellan fell, but in fact his bad advice at Antietam essentially ensured that Lee would manage to save his army from destruction.

REYNOLDS, John Fulton (1820–63)

John Reynolds (see Plate E2) was born in Lancaster, Pennsylvania, on 20 September 1820. After attending Lancaster County Academy he was graduated from West Point in 1841. He served as an artillery officer on the Atlantic coast and in Texas before the Mexican War, in which he was breveted a captain and major for gallant and meritorious conduct. After years of garrison duty, he became Commandant of Cadets at West Point in September 1860, leaving the Academy to become lieutenant-colonel of the 14th US Infantry on 14 May 1861, and a brigadier-general of volunteers on 26 August.

Reynolds commanded the 1st Brigade of Pennsylvania Reserves, raised from excess volunteers from that state, which was assigned to the Army of the Potomac. The men of his brigade had a chance to appreciate Reynolds' coolness in the field during their first experience at the front. Major Evan Woodward, 2nd Reserves, recalled in his history of the Reserves published in 1865: "When we first commenced our retrograde movement many surmises that soon assumed the shape of rumors were set afloat, and as we at that time were incapable of judging of military

movements, they received much credence. An orderly came dashing down the road in search of General Reynolds and almost breathlessly informed him, there were 'forty thousand rebels coming down upon us'. 'Forty thousand old fools', replied the General, 'go back to where you came from'."

Reynolds' brigade was assigned to V Corps in the Peninsula campaign where he, along with his adjutant, was surprised and captured on the night of 27 June 1862. Exchanged on 8 August, he was given command of the 3rd Division of Pennsylvania Reserves in the Second Bull Run (Manassas) campaign. During the Antietam campaign he commanded Pennsylvania militia, and he received command of I Corps of the Army of the Potomac before Fredericksburg (December 1862), at which battle he distinguished himself by his energy and courage.

On 29 November 1862 he was named a major-general of volunteers. Declining to accept command of the Army of the Potomac to replace Hooker, he was appointed by the army's new commander, George Meade, to command the first three corps on the field at Gettysburg. Charles Wainwright noted in his diary: "General Reynolds told me today that the command of this army was offered to him when he was summoned up to Washington a month ago; but he refused it, because, to use his own expression, 'he was unwilling to take Burnside and Hooker's leavings'."

While bringing up the 2nd Wisconsin Infantry to help hold the line at Gettysburg, Reynolds was shot and killed instantly by a Confederate infantryman in a barn on the edge of nearby woodland. He was buried in the main burial plot at Lancaster, only 50 miles away from Gettysburg. He had fallen without receiving a presentation sword, with a blade of the finest Damascus steel, a black onyx grip set with the initials "J.F.R." in diamonds, and a scabbard of pure gold, which had been acquired earlier without a chance for a formal presentation ceremony. The scabbard was engraved, "Presented to Major-general John F. Reynolds, by the enlisted men of the First, Second, Fifth and Eighth regiments of the First Brigade of Pennsylvania, in testimony of their love and admiration. Mechanicsville, June 26th, 1862." The sword was finally presented to Reynolds' sister.

RICKETTS, James Brewerton (1817–87)

James Ricketts was a native of New York City, born on 21 June 1817 into an old family which had settled in New Jersey in the early colonial period. In 1835 he was appointed to West Point, graduating in 1839. Ricketts was commissioned a second lieutenant in the 1st US Artillery and sent to the Canadian frontier. In 1840 he married Harriet Josephine Pierce, who died young, leaving the widowed lieutenant to care for a child. In the Mexican War his artillery battery was assigned to the army under Maj.Gen. Zachary Taylor, fighting at Monterey (20–24 September 1846) and Buena Vista (22–23 February 1847). After the war he was sent to Florida, where he was promoted captain on 3 August 1852. He married Francis Lawrence in 1856; they eventually had five children, of whom only two would grow to adulthood.

The outbreak of the Civil War would find Ricketts as senior captain in the 1st Artillery in command of Company I, which was overrun at First Bull Run (Manassas) on 21 July 1861; badly wounded in the leg, he was taken prisoner. He was exchanged on 20 December and, after leave to

James Ricketts, who as an artillery lieutenant in the 1840s had been left a widower with a small child. He remarried in 1856, and the second Mrs Ricketts – no beauty, and taller than her husband – seems to have taken to army life admirably. The diarist Marsena Patrick, who had known Ricketts from 1835 when they were both at West Point, recorded meeting her in camp in October 1862: "Mrs R. read to me her report of the 2nd Bull Run. She came on here to write it for her husband. She says that from the time she was married, she has always made out his Muster Rolls & Reports... ."

recuperate, on 30 April 1862 he returned to duty and was assigned to command a brigade in the Army of the Rappahannock, being commissioned a brigadier-general of volunteers to rank from 21 July 1862.

On 10 June, Ricketts was named to command the 2nd Division in III Corps, and fought at Cedar Mountain (9 August), Second Bull Run (Manassas – 29–30 August), and Antietam (17 September) – there is some disagreement as to whether or not he was wounded there. At any rate, he left his command on 4 October 1862 and went to Washington, where he served on various commissions and courts-martial until 4 April 1864.

Ricketts was then given command of the 3rd Division, VI Corps; he was offered corps command on John Sedgwick's death but he turned it down, saying that Sedgwick had wanted one of the other divisional commanders to succeed him. The corps was sent to help defend Washington during "Early's Raid", and Ricketts' division fought on the Monocacy River. For his part in the battle, on 1 August 1864 he was commissioned a major-general of volunteers. VI Corps went on to serve in Philip Sheridan's Valley campaign thereafter, and Ricketts was commanding it at Cedar Creek (19 October 1864) when he was badly wounded in the chest and right shoulder. He returned to duty on 7 April 1865, just two days before Lee's surrender at Appomattox.

After the war Ricketts reverted to the rank of major, retiring in January 1867. However, he was so much admired that he continued to serve on courts-martial until 1869. Suffering greatly from the effects of his old wounds, he died on 22 September 1887, and was buried in Arlington National Cemetery.

SCOTT, Winfield (1786–1866)

Winfield Scott (see Plate A1) was quite possibly the greatest soldier the United States ever produced; he had the bad luck, however, to fight in the country's minor wars rather than her major ones. He was born near Petersburg, Virginia, on 13 June 1786, but was orphaned at an early age. He was graduated from William and Mary in 1804 and then studied law. However, rather than practice, he accepted an artillery captain's commission in 1808. He became a lieutenant-colonel in 1812 and adjutant general, ranking as a colonel, in March 1813.

During the War of 1812 he was captured by the British at Queenstown Heights but soon exchanged. Colonel Scott was badly burned in the magazine explosion at Fort George on 27 May 1813 – an operation which he commanded in co-operation with Cdre. Oliver H.Perry. Recovering, Scott became a brigadier-general in early 1814, and won the battle of Chippewa (5 July 1814). He was made a major-general at the end of the war.

After the war Scott traveled in Europe for a time; he prepared military manuals, served in wars with the Seminoles and Creeks, and removed the Cherokees from Georgia. In 1841 he was named general-in-chief of the armies of the United States. Politically Scott was a Whig, and when war with Mexico broke out in 1846 the then-President, Polk, did not want to give him any opportunity to win a victory that might make him a presidential candidate. However, fearing that Zachary Taylor was winning just such victories on the Mexican border, he did finally let Scott command a field army. Scott's landings at Vera Cruz (March 1847) opened a masterly six-month campaign during which he drove west from the coast, captured Mexico City against great odds (14 September 1847), and brought the war to a victorious end. Thereafter Scott was indeed nominated as the Whig presidential candidate in 1852, but lost the election. In 1859 he was the United States commissioner who successfully settled a border dispute between the United States and Britain concerning the Canadian border.

The senior ranks of the pre-war army were characterized by extreme old age, and when the Civil War broke out Scott was well past his prime. Nonetheless, his military mind was still sharp. He wrote to the new administration's Secretary of State on 3 March 1861 that the seceding states could be conquered, but it would take "two or three years, a young and able general – a Wolfe, a Dessaix, or a Hoche – with three hundred thousand disciplined men (kept up to that number), estimating a third for garrison, and the loss of a yet greater number by skirmishes, sieges, battles, and Southern fevers. The destruction of life and property on the other side would be frightful – however perfect the moral discipline of the invaders." At this time Scott was virtually the only individual on the continent who foresaw what such a war would entail; most leaders predicted a short fight with little cost.

However, since it was determined that the Federal government would fight to keep the country together, Scott drew up a plan to win the war. This called for a naval blockade of Southern ports, an army drive to open the Mississippi to split the Confederacy in half, and then the crushing of the rebellion piecemeal. This appreciation, called the "Anaconda Plan", eventually formed the basis of the Federal war effort and, indeed, won the war.

On 30 December 1860, Scott had written to President Buchanan an apology for sending a note with ideas on the national crisis, adding, "It is Sunday, the weather is bad, and General Scott [he habitually referred to himself in the third person] is not well enough even to go to church." Finally, he wrote in his memoirs: "A cripple, unable to walk without assistance for three years, Scott, on retiring from all military

When the Civil War broke out the US Army had only four line officers of general rank: Winfield Scott (illustrated), David E.Twigg, John E.Wool, and William S.Harney. The last named was the only one under 70 years of age, and the only one who had not fought in the War of 1812. Winfield Scott had been directly commissioned into the army by President Jefferson in 1808, and had earned his first general's star in the War of 1812. When the Civil War broke out he had already been the army's commanding general for 20 years.

Scott and his staff in full dress. By 1861 he was 74 years old, grossly fat, and infirm to the point of being unable to ride and hardly able to walk. Nevertheless, the aged victor of Chippewa, Cerro Gordo, Churubusco and Chapultepec designed the strategy that eventually won the Civil War. Possibly America's greatest soldier, Scott lived to see Union victory before dying at West Point in 1866.

duty, October 31, 1861 – being broken down by official labors of from nine to seventeen hours a day, with a decided tendency to vertigo and dropsy, I had the honor to be waited on by President Lincoln, at the head of his Cabinet, who, in a neat and affecting address, took leave of the worn-out soldier." After retirement Winfield Scott went abroad for a short time before settling at West Point, where he died on 29 May 1866, having lived long enough to see victory achieved more or less as he had predicted. He lies in the Post Cemetery at the Academy.

SEDGWICK, John (1813–64)

John Sedgwick (**see Plate H2**) was born at Cornwall Hollow, Connecticut, on 13 September 1813. After early education at a local school and Sharon Academy he went to West Point, where he was graduated in 1837. Thereafter he fought against the Seminoles and participated in the removal of the Cherokees from Georgia. During the Mexican War he served under both Zachary Taylor and Winfield Scott, winning brevets as captain and major.

In 1855 Sedgwick was named major of the new 1st US Cavalry, under Col. Robert E.Lee. When his two immediate superiors resigned to join the Confederate Army in 1861 Sedgwick became the regiment's senior officer. He was commissioned brigadier-general of volunteers on 31 August 1861, commanding a division in II Corps in the Peninsula campaign, where he was badly wounded at Glendale (30 June 1862). Promoted to major-general of volunteers on 4 July 1862, he returned to fight at Antietam (17 September), where he was wounded three times and carried unconscious from the field.

Recovering after only three months, he returned to command IX Corps for a short time before being switched to VI Corps. Sedgwick was then discussed as a potential commander of the Army of the Potomac. On 28 April 1863 Marsena Patrick confided in his diary: "Sedgwick, I fear, is not enough of a General for that position – He is a good honest fellow & that is all. I do not think his officers have much confidence in him."

Sedgwick served at Chancellorsville (1–6 May 1863), but his corps was largely in reserve at Gettysburg (1–3 July 1863). In November 1863 he was given temporary command of both VI and V Corps for an operation in which they captured some 1,700 prisoners, eight flags, and four cannon at Rappahannock Bridge. His corps fought well in the Wilderness (5–6 May 1864). On 9 May, at Spotsylvania, he was warned against exposing himself while posting his troops. His famous reply was, "They couldn't hit an elephant at this distance" – a remark followed immediately by the thud of a bullet hitting him below the left eye and killing him almost instantly. He was buried in Cornwall Hollow. Grant later wrote of him:

"Sedgwick was killed at Spotsylvania before I had an opportunity of forming an estimate of his qualifications as a soldier from personal observation. I had known him in Mexico when both of us were lieutenants, and when our service gave no indication that either of us would ever be equal to the command of a brigade. He stood very high in the army, however, as an officer and a man. He was brave and conscientious. His ambition was not great, and he seemed to dread responsibility. He was willing to do any amount of battling, but always wanted some one else to direct."

John Sedgwick, standing at the center of the bottom step with his hand tucked into his coat, seems never to have desired independent command, but was rapidly promoted to lead a corps in the Peninsula campaign and at Antietam. Frank Haskell wrote: "Sedgwick is quite a heavy man, short, thick-set and muscular, with florid complexion, dark, calm, straight-looking eyes, with full, heavyish features, which, with his eyes, have plenty of animation when he is aroused. He has a magnificent profile, well cut, with the nose and forehead forming almost a straight line, curly, short, chestnut hair and full beard, cut short, with a little gray in it. He dresses carelessly, but can look magnificently when he is well dressed. Like Meade, he looks and is, honest and modest. You might see at once, why his men, because they love him, call him 'Uncle John', not to his face, of course, but among themselves."

SHERIDAN, Philip Henry (1831–88)

Philip Sheridan (**see Plate G3**) was born in Albany, New York, on 6 March 1831, but his family soon moved to Somerset, Ohio. There Sheridan acquired his basic education and clerked in a general store, before being appointed to the West Point class of 1852. While at the Academy he was suspended for a year for fighting with a fellow cadet, hence graduating in 1853, in the bottom third of his class. He was appointed to the 4th US Infantry, and served thereafter on the frontier.

Coming East at the outbreak of the Civil War, he served on Gen. Henry Halleck's staff, before being appointed chief quartermaster and commissary of the Army of Southwest Missouri. Although Sheridan's hard work kept that army well maintained, he and his army commander

Philip Sheridan, an infantry officer before the war, earned command of the 2nd Michigan Cavalry in the West; he did so well in that and higher commands that Grant brought him East to command the cavalry of the Army of the Potomac. Seen here toward the end of the war, Sheridan was supremely self-confident, and with reason. Energetic and ruthless, he would eventually become the US Army's general-in-chief in 1883, living just long enough to receive the rank of full general five years later.

did not see eye to eye. Halleck transferred him back to his own headquarters just before he was court-martialed. There Sheridan caught the eye of some superiors, including William T. Sherman, who saw that he was given command of the 2nd Michigan Cavalry. From this point on Sheridan conducted himself so well that he became one of the bright lights of the Union army.

He was made a brigadier-general of volunteers on 13 September 1862, and saw hard fighting at Perryville (8 October) and Murfreesboro (31 December 1862–3 January 1863). On 16 March 1863 Sheridan was promoted major-general, ranking from the date of Murfreesboro. He commanded a division of XX Corps at Chickamauga (19–20 September 1863), losing some 1,500 men out of the 4,000 under his command. After being besieged in Chattanooga, it was Sheridan's men who stormed Missionary Ridge and hurled the Confederates south (25 November 1863). Ulysses S. Grant, now on the scene in Tennessee, was suitably impressed. When Grant came East he brought in Sheridan to take over the cavalry of the Army of the Potomac, whose previous commanders had lackluster records.

Colonel J.H. Kidd, 6th Michigan Cavalry, described Sheridan as he saw him first when the newcomer assumed this command: "There was nothing about Sheridan's appearance at first glance to mark him as the principal figure in the scene… He was well mounted and sat his horse like a real cavalryman. Though short in stature he did not appear so on horseback. His stirrups were high up, the shortness being of leg and not of trunk. He wore a peculiar style hat not like that of any other officer. He was square of shoulder and there was plenty of room for the display of a major-general's buttons on his broad chest. His face was strong, with a firm jaw, a keen eye, and extraordinary firmness in every lineament. In his manner there was an alertness, evinced rather in look than in movement. Nothing escaped his eye, which was brilliant and searching and at the same time emitted flashes of kindly good nature. When riding among or past his troopers, he had a way of casting quick, comprehensive glances to the right and left and in all directions. He overlooked nothing. One had a feeling that he was under close and critical observation, that Sheridan had his eye on him was mentally taking his measure and would remember and recognize him the next time."

Sheridan's vastly stronger cavalry manhandled the smaller and less well supplied Confederate cavalry in the 1864 campaign, striking deep into the enemy's rear areas. As a result, Grant gave him command of the army sent against Jubal Early in the Shenandoah Valley after Early's "Washington Raid". Sheridan, given orders to clear the Valley once and for all, defeated Early in battle after battle between August 1864 and March 1865. Early struck at Cedar Creek (19 October) while

Sheridan was recognized by his men by the odd little black hat that he wore. On 19 October 1864 he rode along the lines of troops driven from their positions at Cedar Creek by Jubal Early, rallying them to hold and then leading them back into the attack that eventually gained one of the most overwhelming victories of the war.

Sheridan was away in Washington, but the latter returned in the nick of time to rally his troops and virtually destroy the Confederate force.

With the Valley essentially Union, Sheridan was made a major-general in the regular army on 14 November 1864, and rejoined the Army of the Potomac at Petersburg. In command of both the cavalry and an infantry corps, he continued pressing Lee's battered Army of Northern Virginia in the Appomattox campaign of April 1865, preventing the Confederates from joining forces in North Carolina and thus forcing Lee's surrender.

After the war Sheridan was given command of the Fifth Military District in the southwest, where he treated the defeated Southerners so harshly that he was recalled after only six months. Thereafter he held a number of commands, and success in the Cheyenne and Pawnee campaign of 1868–69 brought him promotion to lieutenant-general. In 1870–71 he followed the Franco-Prussian War as an observer. In November 1883 he became general-in-chief of the US Army; named a full general on 1 June 1888, he died only two months later on 5 August at Nonquitt, Massachusetts. He is buried in Arlington National Cemetery.

SICKLES, Daniel Edgar (1819–1914)

Daniel Sickles (**see Plate E3**) was born on 20 October 1819 in New York City. He attended New York University and studied law thereafter. Advancing through Democratic Party politics, he served as the city's corporation counsel, first secretary of the London legation, New York state senator, and US Representative. In 1859 Sickles discovered that his wife was having an affair with Philip Barton Key (son of the author of *The Star Spangled Banner*), whereupon he shot Key dead in broad daylight within yards of the White House. In one of the most sensational trials of the century his counsel, Edwin M.Stanton (later Secretary of War), had Sickles plead temporary insanity, the first time such a defense had ever been offered in the United States. Sickles was acquitted; but it was his defiance of the conventions of the time in taking his tarnished wife back that led to his being ostracized by polite society. In an open letter to the press Sickles declared that he was unaware "of any statute or code of morals which makes it infamous to forgive a woman."

Sickles would never escape his notoriety. Charles Haydon, an officer in the 2nd Michigan, recalled in his diary on 28 February 1862 a conversation with a local civilian near the picket line. "He wanted to know last night if I had heard abt that

Daniel Sickles, a shady New York lawyer and politician who dabbled in militia affairs, was given a general's commission to prove that Democrats supported the Republican administration in the Civil War. Not a professional soldier, he wears here a comfortable, informal version of the general's uniform. Sickles was certainly no coward (he smoked a cigar while being carried from the field with a smashed leg at Gettysburg), and seems to have been an effective leader at a junior level, but he was unfitted to command a corps.

murder in Washington. I asked him what one. "Why abt that – that whats his name – Sickles, who shot a man (Keys) the other day". He overheard some of the pickets talking abt it & having never heard of it before concluded it must be a new thing."

At the outbreak of war Sickles, who had earlier served in the New York militia, resigned from Congress to return to New York and raise the Excelsior Brigade. He was named a brigadier-general of volunteers from 3 September 1861, and was given command of the brigade, thus demonstrating Democratic Party support for the war. Showing great personal bravery and some aptitude for command, he was named a major-general ranking from 29 November 1862. He had command of a division on the Peninsula, at Antietam and Fredericksburg in 1862, and of III Corps at Fredericksburg and Gettysburg.

Very few of his fellow generals thought much of Sickles, however. The waspish Marsena Patrick noted in April 1863: "Sickles & the most of his crew, are poor – very poor concerns in my opinion." Staff officer Frank Haskell, writing about Gettysburg, said that he thought that there "General Sickles supposed he was doing for the best; but he was neither born nor bred a soldier. But one can scarcely tell what may have been the motives of such a man – a politician, and some other things, exclusive of the *Barton Key* affair – a man after show and notoriety, and newspaper fame, and the adulation of the mob!"

At Gettysburg (2 July 1863), dissatisfied with the spot in the line where he had been placed, Sickles advanced his corps to what he saw as better ground. Hardly had he done so when his line was struck by the main Confederate attack. While attempting to rally his men he was shot in the right leg and carried away, nonchalantly smoking a cigar. His leg was amputated, and he never returned to command, although he stayed in the regular army as a major-general until retiring in 1869.

Sickles was later appointed minister to Spain, where he apparently tried to get the two countries into a war over the Spanish capture of an American boat, the *Virginius*, which was running guns into Cuba in 1873. Cooler heads prevailed and a compromise was worked out over his head. He then served in Congress in 1893–95, and was chairman of the New York State Monuments Commission. In 1912 he was removed from the commission for alleged peculation. Slipping into mental illness in his final years, he died at last on 3 May 1914 in New York, and is buried in Arlington National Cemetery.

STONEMAN, George (1822–94)

George Stoneman (**see Plate G1**) was born in Busti, New York, on 22 August 1822. Educated at Jamestown Academy, he went on to West Point where he was graduated in 1846 – George McClellan was a classmate – and was commissioned into the 1st Dragoons. During the Mexican War he was the quartermaster for the Mormon Battalion on its

Although his bungling threatened the integrity of the Union line on the second day of Gettysburg, Sickles was probably most notorious for his private life. He had shot his wife's lover dead in broad daylight, successfully pleaded temporary insanity as a defense at the subsequent trial, and publically forgave his wife thereafter.

George Stoneman, standing center wearing from left shoulder to right hip the sash which indicates that he was serving as general officer of the day. He and his staff pose here in April 1863; a month later he would lead the Army of the Potomac's cavalry off on a fruitless raid during the Chancellorsville campaign.

march from Leavenworth, Kansas, to San Diego, California. At the outbreak of the Civil War he was a captain in the 2nd Cavalry – suffering, as a result of years in the saddle, from a chronic case of hemorrhoids.

Stoneman was quickly placed on McClellan's staff as a major. Commissioned a brigadier-general of volunteers on 13 August 1861, he was named chief of cavalry of the Army of the Potomac (essentially a staff post with no real command functions) when McClellan became army commander. During the Peninsula campaign he actually commanded an infantry division in III Corps, but during much of the campaign he was unable to ride because of sickness, which limited his activities. Even so, made a major-general of volunteers dating from 29 November 1862, he commanded III Corps at Fredericksburg (13 December).

When Hooker took over the Army of the Potomac, Stoneman was made chief of cavalry in a reorganization that made the army's cavalry an effective, independent organization – something he had unsuccessfully urged upon McClellan. He was sent with the Cavalry Corps to raid the rear of the Army of Northern Virginia during the Chancellorsville campaign of May 1863. One fellow general, while awaiting news of the results of a Stoneman raid, said, "I know Stoneman like a book. He will go to the proper spot like a cannon-ball, but when he gets there, like a shell he'll burst." Indeed, the only practical effect of this raid was to deprive the main army of its intelligence-gathering capacities when it needed them most.

After Chancellorsville, and as a result of this poor performance, Stoneman was replaced on 22 May by Alfred Pleasonton. After a time as chief of the Cavalry Bureau in Washington he was returned to a combat command in the winter of 1864. Given XXIII Corps, he actually commanded the Cavalry Corps of the Army of the Ohio during the Atlanta campaign. There his performance was again lackluster. Major-General David Stanley, who had earlier been chief of cavalry of the Army of the Cumberland, told a US Christian Commission delegate that Stoneman was "not competent to command a company."

Stoneman was captured on 31 July 1864 during a raid aimed at freeing prisoners kept at Camp Sumter near Andersonville, Georgia, at the head of two brigades serving as a rear guard to cover the escape of the rest of his command. That October he was exchanged, and commanded troops in eastern Tennessee, northwestern North Carolina, and southwestern Virginia during the last days of the war.

After the war Stoneman was breveted a major-general but assigned as colonel commanding the 21st US Infantry. He commanded the Department of Arizona until retirement in 1871. He then moved to an estate at San Marino, California, serving as railroad commissioner and a term as governor of California in 1882. He died in Buffalo, New York, on 5 September 1894, and was buried at Lakewood, New York.

SUMNER, Edwin Vose (1797–1863)

Edwin Sumner (see Plate B3) was born on 30 January 1797 in Boston. Commissioned directly as a lieutenant in the 2nd US Infantry in 1819, he was made a captain of dragoons in 1833, and served largely on the frontier. In 1846 he was promoted to major and saw service in Mexico, winning two brevets and promotion to lieutenant-colonel in 1848. Named colonel of the 1st Cavalry in 1855, he saw service as commander of Fort Leavenworth during the Kansas troubles.

In 1861 he was named a brigadier-general to replace David Twigg, who had gone south. On the creation of corps in the Army of the Potomac, Sumner was given command of II Corps, which he led in the Peninsula campaign despite receiving two wounds. At first he was not especially effective, McClellan privately writing after the battle of Williamsburg (5 May 1862), "Sumner had proved that he was even a greater fool than I had supposed & had come within an ace of having us defeated." However, after the action at Fair Oaks (31 May–1 June), McClellan wrote to Secretary of War Edwin Stanton that Sumner "displayed the utmost energy in bringing his troops into action, & handled them with the utmost courage in action. He repulsed every attack of the enemy, & drove him wherever he could get at him."

Sumner was breveted a major-general for his service at Fair Oaks on 31 May 1862, and named a major-general of volunteers on 16 July. In August, however, Charles Wainwright recorded a rumor in the army that "General Sumner is said to be very feeble, and failing fast; he has never got over the severe fall from his horse he had last winter." This was not true, as Sumner went on to serve at Antietam (17 September), where there was some complaint that he led his head division like a cavalry colonel rather than a corps commander, who should have been in the rear to supervise. Nevertheless, he was given command of the Left Grand Division, consisting of II and IX Corps, at Fredericksburg in December.

When Hooker was given command of the Army of the Potomac, Sumner asked to be relieved. On his way to his new command, the Department of the Missouri, he died at Syracuse, New York, on 21 March

Edwin Vose Sumner, a veteran professional soldier, was known as "Old Bull" or "Bull Head" after a battle in the Mexican War when a musket ball struck him in the forehead and bounced off, leaving him unhurt. He was no military genius, and his promotion to a corps command was a serious mistake; but the old man's courage at Fair Oaks in May 1862 earned him ungrudging affection. In the words of Col. Charles Wainwright: "He was one of those whom every one must hate to find fault with; yet whose removal from the command of a corps was generally looked on as a relief... ."

1863. He is buried in the Oakwood Cemetery there. Writing after his death, Marsena Patrick noted that Sumner "was a mere soldier – a man of the world & nothing but a man of the world... ." Wainwright was harsher, writing on hearing of Sumner's death: "Owing to his incompetence to fill so large a post as corps commander, we lost the chance to destroy Johnston's army at Williamsburg last May, Antietam was but half a victory; and the heights of Fredericksburg were not secured in December when we first came here.

"But the old soldier was as honest as the day, and simple as a child. The fault was not so much his, as of those who put him and kept him in such a place, while the glorious way in which he pushed across the half-gone bridges to the relief of Keyes at Fair Oaks suffices to cover all his faults."

THE PLATES

The regulation uniform of a general officer was a double-breasted dark blue frock coat with a dark blue velvet standing collar and round "jam pot" cuffs. Major-generals had two rows of nine buttons arranged in groups of three; brigadier-generals had two rows of eight buttons arranged in pairs. Rank was also indicated by transverse shoulder straps of dark blue velvet edged with gold embroidery, bearing two silver stars for a major-general and one for a brigadier-general. The cap or hat badge was a black velvet oval with a gold embroidered wreath enclosing "U.S." in silver Old English lettering. For full dress, gold braid epaulettes were worn, with heavy gold fringes, and two or one silver stars.

The trousers were plain dark blue. The general officers' sword was straight, with a gilt guard, black leather grip wrapped with gilt wire, and a black scabbard with brass mounts. The full dress sword had a silver grip and a brass or steel scabbard. The sword knot was of gold cord with an acorn end. In the field a black leather belt was worn with a plain gilt plate showing the arms of the United States. The full dress belt was of red leather with lengthways gold braid stripes. For dress, and occasionally in the field, a buff silk tasseled sash was worn under the belt.

It should be emphasized that this was the regulation uniform; in practice generals wore variations to suit their needs and preferences.

Irvin McDowell (left) as commander of I Corps, with his army commander George McClellan, before the 1862 Peninsula campaign. Lincoln insisted that McDowell's corps be left behind to protect Washington; McClellan subsequently used this excuse to point the finger of blame at Lincoln for the campaign's failure. Note McDowell's odd forage cap, taller than usual and standing straight like a shako. Distrusting his loyalty, after First Bull Run some soldiers in his army actually claimed that this odd hat marked him out in the field so that Confederates, who knew he was secretly aiding them, would not accidentally shoot him!

Ambrose Burnside wore his old Rhode Island "sack" even when he was a general officer, along with a version of the US Army dress hat stripped of its embroidery and feathers – see Plate C2.

A: MAY 1861

A1: Major-General Commanding the Army Winfield Scott
A2: Major-General Benjamin Butler
A3: Brigadier-General Irvin McDowell

Three generals who were important in the early days of the war meet in Washington to discuss that city's defense. At the outset there was considerable fear that the capital, surrounded by the slave-holding states of Maryland and Virginia, would fall to Southern forces. There were only some 55 officers and men of the Ordnance Corps, and 300 to 400 Marines stationed within city limits, and some of the city's militia companies were of suspect loyalty. Benjamin Butler led some of the first troops from New England to defend Washington; his immediate appointment as a major-general of volunteers was politically motivated. Scott and McDowell, both professional soldiers, were already in the capital. Scott would be obliged to retire on grounds of age and health, while both McDowell and Butler would be disgraced by subsequent failures.

Scott **(A1)**, known to his men as "Old Fuss and Feathers", and Butler both preferred fanciful variations on regulation dress; note the heavy gold embroidery on the fall collar and cuffs affected by Scott. Unique in his rank as Major-General Commanding the Army, Scott wore its three silver stars on his epaulettes, the center star larger than the other two. Eventually the three-star insignia would be adopted for use by Ulysses S.Grant when he was named a lieutenant-general, and would survive as a lieutenant-general's rank insignia to this day. Butler **(A2)** has the regulation stand collar, but also sports gold embroidery along its top and front edges; portraits show at least two variations of this style. McDowell **(A3)** preferred regulation dress, but was unmistakable for his unique style of cap – see accompanying photograph.

B: AUGUST 1862

B1: Major-General John Pope
B2: Major-General Fitz John Porter
B3: Major-General Edwin Sumner

Toward the end of his disastrous Second Bull Run (Manassas) campaign, John Pope, commanding the Army of Virginia, meets two Army of the Potomac corps commanders, while in the background exhausted men of John Gibbon's "Iron Brigade" prepare their suppers. All three wear the regulation uniform for major-generals, differenced only by their personal choice of headgear; Porter **(B2)** wears the so-called "McClellan" style forage cap, the other two broad-brimmed slouch hats with gold cord and acorns, Sumner's **(B3)** without a badge. Pope would later have Porter court-martialed; he was always bitter about what he believed was the desire of senior officers of the Army of the Potomac to see him beaten in the field. He wrote years later: "It was the knowledge of this feeling and the open exultation of Franklin and other officers of rank in his corps over the fact that their comrades had been worsted in the battle of the day before which induced me to recommend that the army be drawn back to the intrenchments around Washington and there thoroughly reorganized. There did not appear to me to be any hope of success for that army while such a feeling prevailed among so many of its higher officers."

C: NOVEMBER 1862
C1: Major-General George McClellan
C2: Major-General Ambrose Burnside
C3: Brigadier-General Henry Hunt

McClellan turns over command of the Army of the Potomac to Ambrose Burnside, 7 November 1862. It was well after dark when Burnside arrived with Gen. Catharinus Buckingham, who had been on duty at the War Department at the time and personally delivered the orders from the Secretary of War to Burnside; a newspaper sketch artist caught McClellan and Burnside in discussion outside the former's headquarters tent. McClellan, who had constantly misread Abraham Lincoln, was shocked to receive orders to hand over command; but he wisely disregarded the excitable advice of his supporters in the army to ignore them. Instead he retired to Trenton, New Jersey (which one wag said was the only city he was able to take). McClellan described the event in a letter to his wife written at 11.30pm that night:

"No cause is given. I am ordered to turn over the command immediately & repair to Trenton N.J. & on my arrival there to report by telegraph for future orders!! Poor Burn feels dreadfully, almost crazy – I am sorry for him, & he never showed himself a better man or truer friend than now. Of course I was much surprised – but as I read the order in the presence of Genl Buckingham, I am sure that not a muscle quivered nor was the slightest expression of feeling visible on my face, which he watched closely. They shall not have that triumph. They have made a great mistake – alas for my poor country – I know in my innermost heart she never had a truer servant. I have informally turned over the command to Burnside – but will go tomorrow to Warrenton with him, & perhaps remain a day or two there in order to give him all the information in my power."

While McClellan (C1) wears entirely regulation uniform with the style of forage cap named after him and tall black riding boots, Burnside (C2) still wears his old Rhode Island militia overshirt, which he preferred to wear in the field even as an army commander; the other details of his costume are also from photographs. Inside the tent, Gen.Hunt (C3), the army's brilliant chief of artillery, wears a custom-made single-breasted fatigue blouse with a fall collar, and a black rubberized rain cover on his cap.

D: MAY 1863
D1: Major-General Joseph Hooker
D2: Major-General Darius Couch
D3: Major-General William Franklin

Hooker, Burnside's successor as commander of the Army of the Potomac, meets with his second in command, Couch, and the commander of VI Corps, Franklin, before the Chancellorsville campaign, as his troops form up to get under way; the infantry regiment in the background is led by its fife and drum corps. Note the regulation horse furniture for a general officer (D1). All three generals wear regulation uniform, but note that Couch (D2) is shown in photographs with major-general's shoulder straps applied to his old brigadier-general's coat.

During the campaign Darius Couch would become disgusted with Hooker, who he believed to have lost all confidence and who, instead of following the original plan to burst out of the Wilderness in Lee's rear, withdrew to defensive lines around the Chancellor House, only to meet decisive defeat there.

E: JUNE 1863
E1: Major-General George Meade
E2: Major-General John Reynolds
E3: Major-General Daniel Sickles

Just before Gettysburg, the new Army of the Potomac commander Gen.Meade discusses Lee's invasion of Pennsylvania with Reynolds, commander of I Corps, and Sickles, commander of III Corps; in the background troops have set up an evening camp. Meade gave Reynolds command of all the troops on the scene on the first day of the battle, but Reynolds was killed while scouting that afternoon. Sickles would put the Union line at risk through his unauthorized movement of his command just before the Confederates struck on the second day; Gettysburg would cost him a leg, but he would live to a ripe old age, surrounded by an aura of rascality. All three generals are taken from photographs. Note Sickles' (E3) open single-breasted coat worn over a waistcoat, with his major-general's stars worn on shoulder straps lacking the regulation gold borders. Many of Meade's personal effects survive in the Civil War Library & Museum, Philadelphia, PA; he was portrayed with a dress sword belt of red leather with gold braid stripes.

F: II CORPS COMMANDERS, AUTUMN 1864
F1: Major-General Winfield Scott Hancock
F2: Brigadier-General Francis Barlow
F3: Brigadier-General John Gibbon

The greatly admired Gen. Hancock sits with two of the divisional commanders of his II Corps in 1864 – after a famous photograph (from which we have omitted Maj.Gen. David Birney) of a group of generals all of whom had been wounded at Gettysburg the previous year. Hancock (F1), whose life was despaired of at one point, wears regulation uniform but without a hat badge. Barlow (F2) had been so badly wounded that he was left for dead, but had recovered enough to rejoin the army for the 1864 campaign. He wears the plain, single-breasted short jacket preferred as more comfortable than a frock coat in the saddle, and a standard issue cavalry saber. Instead of the regulation "U.S." he displays the single silver star of his rank on the front of his issue forage cap. Gibbon (F3), an artilleryman before the war and author of *The Artillerist's Manual* while an instructor at West Point, was the second commander of the "Iron Brigade" of troops from Wisconsin, Indiana, and Michigan. Here he wears a custom-made version of the fatigue blouse or "sack coat" and the single star of brigadier-general – he was promoted major-general from early June. Note the use of civilian shirts under the uniform coats.

G: CAVALRY COMMANDERS OF THE ARMY OF THE POTOMAC
G1: Brigadier-General George Stoneman
G2: Major-General Alfred Pleasonton
G3: Major-General Philip Sheridan

The cavalry of the Army of the Potomac was commanded successively by these three officers, all of whom wear largely regulation uniform for their rank, and carry plain cavalry sabers. The only striking detail is Sheridan's (G3) odd hat, a small black felt rather resembling a straw boater in outline. Neither Pleasonton nor Stoneman proved very successful in the field; but Stoneman did successfully lobby to make the

Cavalry Corps a separate, independent command instead of splitting it up among various infantry corps – an important factor in its later success under Philip Sheridan. By the time Sheridan took command the quality of the Confederate cavalry, in terms of horses, weapons, and numbers, was so relatively poor that he easily outfought them in most engagements.

H: PETERSBURG, MAY 1864
H1: Major-General Andrew Humphreys
H2: Major-General John Sedgwick
H3: Major-General Joshua Chamberlain

In front of Army of the Potomac headquarters in the field, Gen. Chamberlain reports to the army chief-of-staff, Gen. Humphreys. Andrew Humphreys made the successful transition from topographical engineer to unit commander to army chief-of-staff, where his work was quite successful, and then to corps commander, marking him as a superior

soldier. He wears regulation uniform **(H1)** with his trousers outside his boots.

John Sedgwick **(H2)** was one of the army's most beloved corps commanders; although his superiors found him unwilling to assume independent command responsibility, his death at Spotsylvania on 9 May was a real blow to the army. His saddle and other effects are preseved in the West Point Museum; a photograph shows him with his coat worn open at the neck. The Maine general Joshua Chamberlain **(H3)**, the hero of Little Round Top, is illustrated here resplendent in as near to a dress uniform as would be worn in the field, where epaulettes were virtually never seen; he has the general's buff sash beneath his plain black belt supporting a staff officer's sword. This remarkable officer became more widely known through the pages of Michael Shaara's Pulitzer prize-winning 1975 novel *The Killer Angels*, which later formed the basis for the 1993 feature film *Gettysburg*.

Joseph Hooker – see Plate D1 – certainly looked the part of a general. His estimation of his own worth was not shared by his contemporaries such as John Gibbon and Ulysses Grant, however; and when he threatened to resign after being passed over for a command, Gen.Sherman calmly let this disloyal subordinate go.

OPPOSITE **A famous 1864 photograph of Winfield Scott Hancock as commander of II Corps (seated), with, left to right, his divisional commanders Brig.Gen. Francis Barlow, Maj.Gen. David Birney, and Brig.Gen. John Gibbon – cf Plate F.**

INDEX

References to illustrations are shown in **bold**. Plates are shown with page and caption locators in brackets.

COMPANION SERIES FROM OSPREY

ESSENTIAL HISTORIES
Concise studies of the motives, methods and repercussions of human conflict, spanning history from ancient times to the present day. Each volume studies one major war or arena of war, providing an indispensable guide to the fighting itself, the people involved, and its lasting impact on the world around it.

CAMPAIGN
Accounts of history's greatest conflicts, detailing the command strategies, tactics, movements and actions of the opposing forces throughout the crucial stages of each campaign. Full-color battle scenes, 3-dimensional 'bird's-eye views', photographs and battle maps guide the reader through each engagement from its origins to its conclusion.

ORDER OF BATTLE
The greatest battles in history, featuring unit-by-unit examinations of the troops and their movements as well as analysis of the commanders' original objectives and actual achievements. Color maps including a large fold-out base map, organizational diagrams and photographs help the reader to trace the course of the fighting in unprecedented detail.

MEN-AT-ARMS
The uniforms, equipment, insignia, history and organization of the world's military forces from earliest times to the present day. Authoritative text and full-color artwork, photographs and diagrams bring over 5,000 years of history vividly to life.

NEW VANGUARD
The design, development, operation and history of the machinery of warfare through the ages. Photographs, full-color artwork and cutaway drawings support detailed examinations of the most significant mechanical innovations in the history of human conflict.

WARRIOR
Insights into the daily lives of history's fighting men and women, past and present, detailing their motivation, training, tactics, weaponry and experiences. Meticulously researched narrative and full-color artwork, photographs, and scenes of battle and daily life provide detailed accounts of the experiences of combatants through the ages.

AIRCRAFT OF THE ACES
Portraits of the elite pilots of the 20th century's major air campaigns, including unique interviews with surviving aces. Unit listings, scale plans and full-color artwork combine with the best archival photography available to provide a detailed insight into the experience of war in the air.

COMBAT AIRCRAFT
The world's greatest military aircraft and combat units and their crews, examined in detail. Each exploration of the leading technology, men and machines of aviation history is supported by unit listings and other data, artwork, scale plans, and archival photography.